TEACHER'S DICTATION MANUAL
IN
EAR TRAINING

▲

SECOND EDITION

Bruce Benward
University of Wisconsin

WM. C. BROWN COMPANY PUBLISHERS
Dubuque, Iowa

MUSIC SERIES

Consulting Editor
Frederick W. Westphal
Sacramento State College

Copyright © 1961 by
Bruce Benward

Copyright © 1969 by
Wm. C. Brown Company Publishers

ISBN 0−697−03578−6

Second Printing, 1971

Printed in the United States of America

PREFACE

College theory courses in the United States are divided into two types: (1) those that offer an *integrated* course under one title, the course consisting of training in harmony (written), ear training, sightsinging, and keyboard harmony, all closely interwoven and interrelated; (2) those that offer *separate* courses in each of the above areas.

A variety of excellent texts have been written in all areas of music theory except that of ear training. In the past instructors have arbitrarily drawn material for the ear training courses from texts adopted for sightsinging and from other happen-chance sources. Realizing the general neglect of the area and the fact that too often the material used in ear training is a haphazard selection of unrelated and poorly chosen exercises, the author of this text has prepared a complete freshman college ear training course which may be used in a flexible manner to fill the need for a precise and sound approach to this most important facet of musical discipline.

Some of the advantages of this book include:

1. The book may be used as a programmed text. Answers as well as all dictated material are included in TEACHER'S DICTATION MANUAL.
2. A large number of exercises in the text are obtainable on improved tapes. Thus the instructor may:
    a. Use the book entirely as a programmed text with students taking dictation entirely from recorded tapes. Since the TEACHER'S DICTATION MANUAL contains all dictated material as well as the CORRECT ANSWERS to all exercises, copies may be placed near the recorded material so the student can check his answers as he finishes each dictation exercise.
    b. Use the book for class and the recorded material as supplementary assignments for slow students. Outside of class these students may set their own pace, hear each exercise a number of times using the recorded tapes, and immediately check their answers with the TEACHER'S DICTATION MANUAL. Only about half the material found in this text is recorded. Thus, the instructor can dictate directly from the piano in class using the exercises which are not recorded.
    c. The instructor, through lack of facilities or for pedagogical reason, may wish to use the book only in class. In this manner it is equally effective and may be used with great success.
3. Conveniently organized and carefully graded material *specifically* chosen for dictation.
4. Covers areas of melody, harmony, and rhythm with equal emphasis on each.
5. Essentially designed as a *complete* freshman college course in ear training. Eliminates need of searching for additional supplementary material.
6. This text can be used in collaboration with *any* combination of textbooks in harmony, sightsinging, and keyboard harmony.
7. Since it is complete and self sufficient as an ear training text it is particularly desirable for inexperienced as well as experienced instructors of theory.

8. Particularly designed to cover the first year of ear training as recommended by the National Association of Schools of Music.
9. Expands the various types of dictation possible. Eliminates the danger of stereotyped exercises given day in and day out.

Includes the following dictation types:

    a. Multiple choice.
    b. Correction of errors.
    c. Completion of partially written exercises.
    d. Recognition of devices.
    e. Interval identification.
    f. Exercises with a minimum of explanation provided.
    g. Contrapuntal exercises—emphasis on harmonic intervals produced.
    h. Contrapuntal exercises—emphasis on writing the melodies.
    i. Harmonic arrangement exercises.
    j. Some exercises in contemporary melodic styles.
    k. Exercises which involve musical notation as well as those which involve only auditory judgment.

The TEACHER'S DICTATION MANUAL is intended to be used in connection with the WORKBOOK IN EAR TRAINING (for students), and the recorded TAPES FOR EAR TRAINING. The material covered in this book represents an entire balanced course in ear training for the college freshman student. The book is divided into three main sections: (1) Melody Units, (2) Harmony Units, (3) Rhythm Units, and for best results dictation in all three should be given concurrently, that is, students should be given assignments in Melody Unit No. 1, Harmony Unit No. 1, and Rhythm Unit No. 1 during the first week of the semester and continue in the same manner through the freshman year. For more detailed information the following breakdown may be helpful:

I. MELODY UNITS
    A. 16 units or lessons, one for each two weeks of a 32-week school year. Most colleges operate on this basis, and these units cover the entire first year of a theory course.

        1. Each of the 16 units is divided into three or four sections which represent different types of drills (previously mentioned).
            a. Within each short set of drills some of the exercises are very simple—all students should be able to answer these; however, there are also exercises which will challenge even the best students. This is done to insure that the Workbook will reach all categories of students from mediocre to brilliant.

II. HARMONY UNITS
    A. 16 graded units or lessons, one for each two weeks of a 32-week school year. These cover the first year of harmony study. All triads in all inversions and the dominant seventh chord are introduced. This is roughly the scope of most first year theory textbooks in Harmony. These units follow very closely the written material taken up by the more popular first year theory texts.

        1. Each of the 16 units is divided into three or four sections which present various different types of drills to include all possible facets of approach.
            a. Within each short set or section some of the exercises are very simple—well within the scope of all students; however, there are also exercises which will challenge even the best students.

III. RHYTHM UNITS
  A. 16 graded units, one for each two weeks of a 32-week school year. These cover practically all rhythmic problems found in actual music. This is roughly the scope of most first year sight singing books now in use.

  1. Each of the 16 units is divided into three or four sections which represent different types of drills to include all facets of approach.
     a. Within each section the exercises are graded from easy to difficult so that all students in the class will be challenged.

It will be noted further throughout the entire book that a clear division is made between the recorded exercises and the unrecorded exercises. Although helpful and extremely more practical, the use of records is by no means a positive requirement for the successful conclusion of the material contained in this book. For those instructors who for one reason or another do not wish to use the records or tapes the organization and intent of the book is not in the least altered. The records add flexibility and save time in class work, but they are by no means a necessity to the success of this ear training course.

INTRODUCTION

MELODY UNITS
      In order to introduce the discipline of melodic dictation it is wise to start with the scale and scale formations. The following scale drills should begin on the first day of class and should be continued until the students have mastered the material. A few days after the scale drills have been instituted the first Melody Unit may be assigned. Triad drills should be taken up almost simultaneously with scale drills, but these will be explained and illustrated in the section of this book entitled "Harmony Units."

SCALE DRILLS
1. Have students become familiar with scales and scale formations by singing the scale numbers (or "do" syllables).
   a. At first students sing major and three forms of the minor scales beginning on the tonic note.
   b. As the student gains familiarity with scales starting on the tonic tone the instructor should gradually introduce the singing of the scales beginning on other tones than the tonic.
   c. When the student has gained a firm grasp of scales and scale pattern sounds, the instructor should begin to call out various scale steps to be sung. (The tonic degree should always introduce such a drill):
   Instructor plays:

   Instructor then asks students to sing the fifth degree of the major scale. Student then sings:

   After a short time this procedure can be expanded. The instructor may again play the "G" as listed above and ask the student to respond with the degrees 4 - 2 - 5 - 1. The student then sings:

   This drill procedure can be carried on to the limit of the students' or classes' capacity. For instance the instructor may play:

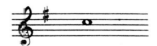

He announces that this is the fourth degree of a major scale. He then asks the students to sing 7 - 1 - 6 - 3 - 5 - 1, and the students respond by singing:

The above drills are recommended to orient the student to the scales and scale pattern sounds. These should be initiated at the very beginning of the course in ear training. After a few days of such drills the instructor can safely begin the main body of the melodic dictation material as set forth in this text. The first few exercises are quite simple and should provide no difficulty even to the average or below average student.

Of course the portions of the book which are recorded are intended to be used as drill outside the classroom. However, it should never be assumed that the student will immediately discover the most efficient and practical method of taking dictation. Much can be done by the instructor in class to assist the student in effecting an orderly and well organized procedure of dictation.

Two possible procedures are suggested in making the material in this book most effective.

I. FIRST SUGGESTED PROCEDURE:
   A. Introduce each new unit in class with an exercise or two taken from that unit. Stress continually:

      1. Student should memorize the sound of the dictated passage before trying to write it down. This he can LEARN to do right in class if the instructor will play over short sections and give the student an opportunity to sing them back to the instructor before writing them down on paper. Students can never learn to write down the music as fast as — *Yes, they can!* it is dictated, and indeed he should not be allowed to proceed in this direction. As the difficulty and length of the exercises increase from unit to unit, the student will find himself more hopelessly lost if he persists in trying to write the notes on score paper as fast as they are dictated.

   B. After the student has learned the most successful method of taking down dictation in class the instructor makes an outside assignment of the entire recorded portion of the unit. The student then has an opportunity to test his newly acquired skill in taking dictation—this time from records at a controlled speed. If he requires more frequent listenings he should indulge himself in these, but should always strive to increase his perception to the point that he needs only the number of replayings given on the record.

   C. At the next meeting of the class the instructor should check the student's outside dictation by giving the correct answers in class. The instructor may at this point wish to give a short test to determine the success of the outside drill. Sufficient additional exercises are available in each unit to provide material for this test. The test material may be selected from any of the "unrecorded" portion of the unit not previously used on the first day to illustrate or introduce the dictation procedure.

II. SECOND SUGGESTED PROCEDURE:
   A. Assign the student a recorded unit of dictation without any advance preparation in class.
   B. At the next class meeting go over the recorded material in class and check the accuracy of each student's dictation. If any of the students indicate difficulty with the material the instructor should experiment with slowing down the speed of dictation, giving the students more time to complete

their solutions, and emphasize the proper steps (previously discussed) to achieve the best results. If class time permits a short test may be administered to find out if better results are being obtained.

Undoubtedly the first procedure is more thorough and gets better results than the second, but it is admittedly the most time consuming. Some instructors may find that the second procedure is almost a necessity in order to cover the semester's material in the time allotted.

The material covered in this book is presumed to be geared to the average student with average capabilities and average response. Instructors who find themselves with an exceptional group of students may alter the difficulty of any particular exercise through the following procedures:

1. *The Speed of Dictation.* This is a major factor in establishing the level of difficulty for any particular exercise. If the speed is reduced, the exercise becomes easier, and if the speed is increased the exercise becomes more difficult. So, any particular exercise can be altered to fit any given situation by increasing or decreasing the dictation speed.

2. *The Number of Repetitions.* This is another major factor in establishing the level of difficulty. If the instructor finds that a particular exercise is too difficult for a particular group of students (when the recommended number of repetitions are used), he can automatically down-grade the exercise by increasing the number of repetitions. Students, themselves, will tend to use this procedure in using the recorded material, and the principle may be used to good advantage by the instructor in class.

3. *The Length of Dictated Phrase.* The smaller the phrase the easier is the dictation. In a classroom drill situation the instructor should start with very short (but meaningful) units, perhaps of two measures only, and work toward longer units. This increases memory retainment, and encourages students continually to think in terms of larger and larger musical units.

4. *The Amount of Time Allotted to the Solution of an Exercise (After It Has Been Dictated).* This to a lesser degree is also a determining factor in the difficulty level of any particular exercise. The instructor will find that he can alter the dictation difficulty by increasing or decreasing the amount of time he gives the student to work on the exercise *after* he has finished dictating it.

An illustration of the above four principles is shown here. The exercise is Melody Unit No. 1, Section C, Exercise 1:

FOR AN INEXPERIENCED CLASS:

1. Speed of dictation: MM ♩ = 40
2. Number of repetitions: 3
3. Length of dictated unit: one measure at a time
4. Time allotted to solution: 2 minutes

FOR AN AVERAGE CLASS:

1. Speed of dictation: MM ♩ = 92
2. Number of repetitions: 2
3. Length of dictated unit: three measures at a time
4. Time allotted to solution: 1 minute

FOR AN HONORS CLASS:

1. Speed of dictation: MM ♩ = 208
2. Number of repetitions: 1
3. Length of dictated unit: three measures at a time
4. Time allotted to solution: 30 seconds

If any one particular type of exercise is used to the exclusion of all others the student soon adjusts to this one type of dictation. He is not challenged to adapt his skills to other facets of the discipline, and thereby his ear training ability becomes stereotyped and inflexible. This book introduces many types of melodic dictation exercises. It is important that a student be able to write an entire melody from dictation, but it is also important and possibly more practical that he be able to recognize errors in a printed score. For this reason many exercises are included which will force the student to adapt himself to make practical his ear training skill. Some of the exercise types in this book will prove easy for one student and difficult for another with the same ability. It is the hope that this more universal approach will keep the student constantly alert to the new presentations and not allow him to fall into the rut of learning *one* dictation procedure which he can solve in an almost automatic manner without having to use his conscious thought processes.

TABLE OF CONTENTS

MELODY UNIT NO. 1

A. SCALEWISE MELODIES—SAME OR DIFFERENT

To the Student: You will hear two short melodies with a pause between them. In some exercises the pitches in both melodies will be the same, in others the pitches will be altered in the second melody. Disregard rhythmic differences. Rhythm is not a factor in these exercises.

Directions:
1. Mark SAME if the pitches of the second melody are the same as those of the first.
2. Mark DIFFERENT if any of the pitches of the second melody are different from those of the first.

To the Teacher: Play the first melody of each exercise and after a slight pause play the second. A tempo of 100 per quarter note is suggested, but a slower or faster tempo may be taken at the discretion of the instructor.

1a. / 1b.   Same

2a. / 2b.   Different

3a. / 3b.   Different

4a. / 4b.   Same

5a. / 5b.   Different

6a. / 3b.   Different

7a. / 7b.   Same

MELODY UNIT NO. 1

Workbook Page 1

B. SCALEWISE MELODIES

To the Student: Each exercise consists of three written melodies (a, b, c), ONE of which will be played by the instructor.

Directions: Place a circle around the letter designating the melody played by the instructor.

To the Teacher: Play each of the following melodies at a comfortable tempo and in a continuous fashion (without interruption). The student should be encouraged to hear these melodies as a unit.

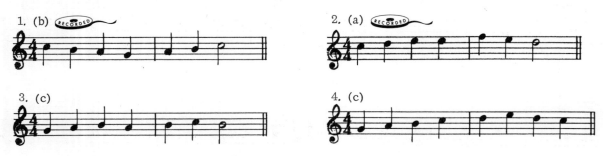

MELODY UNIT NO. 1

C. SCALEWISE MELODIES

To the Student: In each exercise below you are given the key signature, the time signature, and the first note only. You will hear a melodic phrase.

Directions: Complete the phrase on the staff in notation.

To the Teacher:

Procedure:

1. Have the students sing the scale of each exercise.
2. Play the exercise once or twice.
3. Have the students sing the exercise as you played it—they should be encouraged to memorize longer and longer units.
4. When the students can sing the exercise correctly, they are ready to write it on the staff.
5. If you have students who are unable to sing the melody (memorize it), have them come to the piano and play it (from memory). Frequently students will be able to repeat the melody on the piano when they are unable to sing it. This procedure sometimes strengthens students' visual image and improves their ability to write the melody on the staff.

The first note of each exercise is provided in the student workbook.

MELODY UNIT NO. 1

D. INTERVALS OF THE P 8, P 4, M 7, M 2

To the Student: The teacher will play an interval. The first note of the interval is given and is written on the staff for you.

Numbers 1 through 30—The given note is the *lower* note of the interval.

Numbers 31 through 60—The given note is the *upper* note of the interval.

Directions:
1. Write the name of the interval in the space provided.
2. Write the other note of the interval on the staff.

To the Teacher: Play the first note (whole note) then the second note (unstemmed black note). Have the students sing both notes immediately. Repeat the procedure if necessary.

Some teachers prefer to have the students associate each interval with a particular well known composition. The first two notes of the Wedding March by Wagner form a Perfect 4th. The first two notes of Oh Suzanna form a Major 2nd, and so on. In the early stages of learning intervals this practice is effective, but later on instant recognition is seriously impaired—the procedure is too cumbersome.

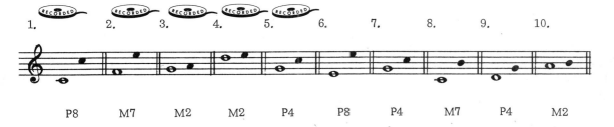

5

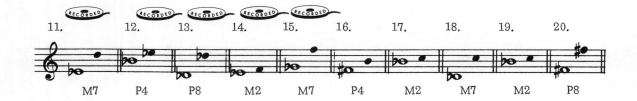

11. M7　12. P4　13. P8　14. M2　15. M7　16. P4　17. M2　18. M7　19. M2　20. P8

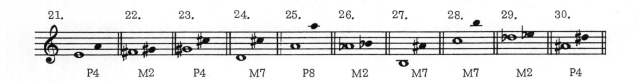

21. P4　22. M2　23. P4　24. M7　25. P8　26. M2　27. M7　28. M7　29. M2　30. P4

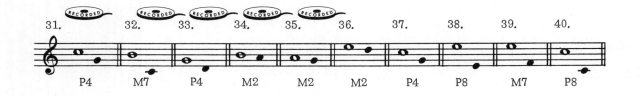

31. P4　32. M7　33. P4　34. M2　35. M2　36. M2　37. P4　38. P8　39. M7　40. P8

41. M2　42. P4　43. M7　44. P8　45. P4　46. M7　47. M2　48. M2　49. P4　50. P8

51. P4　52. M2　53. P8　54. M7　55. M2　56. M7　57. P4　58. M2　59. P8　60. P4

MELODY UNIT NO. 2

A. RECOGNITION OF NON-DIATONIC NOTES

To the Student: Each exercise is a short melodic phrase in the key of C major. One note in Exercises 1-5 and two notes in Exercises 6-10 are not diatonic (in this instance not a note in the C major scale). Before beginning the dictation the instructor will play the C major scale—sing it when he finishes.

Directions:
Exercises 1 through 5—Circle the number indicating the ONE non-diatonic note.
Exercises 6 through 10—Circle the numbers indicating the TWO non-diatonic notes.

To the Teacher:
1. Play the C major scale shown below.
2. Have the students sing it immediately.
3. Then, play the exercise (once or twice) about 100 MM.
4. Have the students sing the melody until they have it memorized.
5. Then, have the students sing the scale again and determine which notes of the melody are not found in the scale.
6. The students are then ready to write their answers on paper.

The circles indicate the correct answers.

MELODY UNIT NO. 2

B. MELODIES INVOLVING LEAPS OUTLINING THE TONIC TRIAD

To the Student: The following melodies contain errors in pitch. You will hear the melody played correctly. Determine the errors in pitch notation.

Directions: Place a circle around each note that is different in pitch from that which is played.

To the Teacher: Play each of the following melodies at a slow but steady tempo. Repeat each melody as few times as necessary for proper perception. Have the students sing the correct melody (as played), then the melody as printed.

The "×"s indicate the notes the students are to circle.

MELODY UNIT NO. 2

C. MELODIES INVOLVING LEAPS OUTLINING THE TONIC TRIADS

To the Student: In each exercise below you are given the key signature, the time signature, and the first note only. Exercises No. 29 through 36 provide an occasional other note. You will hear a melodic phrase.

Directions: Complete the phrase on the staff in notation.

To the Teacher:
Procedure:
1. Have the students sing the scale of each exercise.
2. Play the exercise once or twice.
3. Have the students sing the exercise as you played it—they should be encouraged to memorize longer and longer units.
4. When the students can sing the exercise correctly, they are ready to write it on the staff.

Only the first note of all exercises, nos. 1-28 is given in the student workbook.

The "×" is used in exercises, nos. 29-34 to indicate the notes the students must supply.

34.

35.

36.

MELODY UNIT NO. 2

D. INTERVALS OF THE m 2, M 3, TRITONE (T), M 6

To the Student: The teacher will play an interval. The first note of the interval is given and is written on the staff for you.

Numbers 1 through 30—The given note is the *lower* note of the interval.
Numbers 31 through 60—The given note is the *upper* note of the interval.

Directions:
1. Write the name of the interval in the space provided.
2. Write the other note of the interval on the staff.

To the Teacher: Play the first note (whole note) then the second note (unstemmed black note). Have the students sing both notes immediately. Repeat the procedure if necessary.

Some teachers prefer to have the students associate each interval with a particular well known composition. The first two notes of "My Bonnie Lies Over the Ocean" form the interval of a Major 6th. In the early stages of learning intervals this practice is effective, but later on instant recognition is seriously impaired—the procedure is too cumbersome.

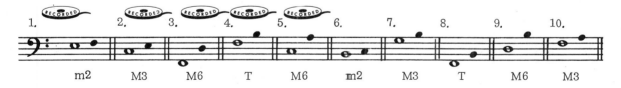

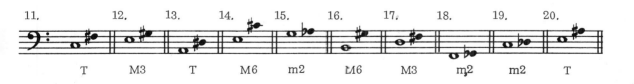

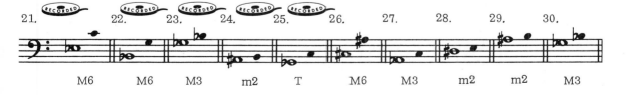

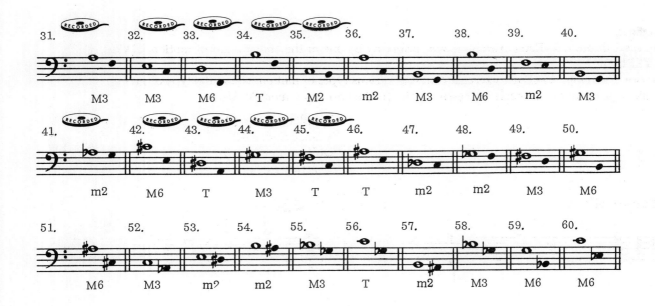

31. 32. 33. 34. 35. 36. 37. 38. 39. 40.

M3   M3   M6   T   M2   m2   M3   M6   m2   M3

41. 42. 43. 44. 45. 46. 47. 48. 49. 50.

m2   M6   T   M3   T   T   m2   m2   M3   M6

51. 52. 53. 54. 55. 56. 57. 58. 59. 60.

M6   M3   m2   m2   M3   T   m2   M3   M6   M6

Workbook Page 11

MELODY UNIT NO. 2
E. PARALLEL, SIMILAR, OBLIQUE, AND CONTRARY MOTION

To the Student: Each exercise consists of two voices progressing by one of the types of motion stated below.
The types are:

PARALLEL MOTION—two voices moving in the same direction keeping the same general harmonic interval:

6   6   3   3   4   4

SIMILAR MOTION—two voices moving (up or down) in the same direction but not by the same harmonic interval:

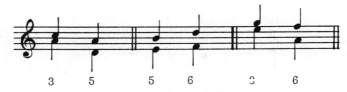

3   5   5   6   3   6

OBLIQUE MOTION—two voices in which one voice repeats the same pitch while the other voice moves:

5   6   5   8   3   6

CONTRARY MOTION—two voices moving in opposite directions:

6   8   8   3   3   8

Directions:

Exercises 1 through 5—Each exercise moves primarily by one of the above types of motion. NAME THE TYPE OF MOTION.

Exercises 6 through 15—Each exercise contains various types of motion. Name the type of motion which takes place between each successive note in the two voice melody. Use:

Parallel motion—P
Similar motion—S
Oblique motion—O
Contrary motion—C

13

MELODY UNIT NO. 3
A. DIATONIC MELODIES OUTLINING LEAPS BETWEEN FACTORS OF THE I AND V TRIADS

To the Student: In each exercise below you are given the key signature, the time signature, and the first note only. You will hear a melodic phrase.

Directions: Complete the phrase on the staff in notation.

To the Teacher: Use the same procedure as with Melody Unit No. 1, Section C. Make sure the students can sing the exercise before writing it on paper.
The first note of each exercise is given in the student workbook.

MELODY UNIT NO. 3

B. DIATONIC MELODIES OUTLINING LEAPS BETWEEN FACTORS OF THE I AND V TRIADS

To the Student: As you hear the melody played in each exercise determine which of the three possibilities is the one the instructor performs.

Directions: Place a circle around the letter designating the melody played by the instructor.

To the Teacher: Play each of the following melodies at a comfortable tempo—somewhat faster than that used for dictating melodies.

11. (c)

12. (a)

MELODY UNIT NO. 3
C. INTERVALS FORMED BY TWO MELODIC LINES

To the Student: Each exercise below consists of four harmonic intervals. These will be played slowly in succession by the teacher. Listen carefully to each interval formed.

    Directions: Write the name of the interval formed in the blanks below. It is not necessary to name the *quality* of the interval—only the interval itself.

    For example, in the first exercise the teacher plays:

You write in the blanks: 8   7   6   5

To the Teacher: Play each interval at the rate of about one per second, slower if necessary. As the students become more proficient at recognizing intervals quickly, ask them to relate the answers verbally.

    Since the emphasis in these exercises is speed the student is asked to name the interval but not the quality of the interval. If you think your students can also name the interval quality as well this is even more desirable. They would then answer (above) P 8, M 7, M 6, P 5 rather than just 8, 7, 6, 5.

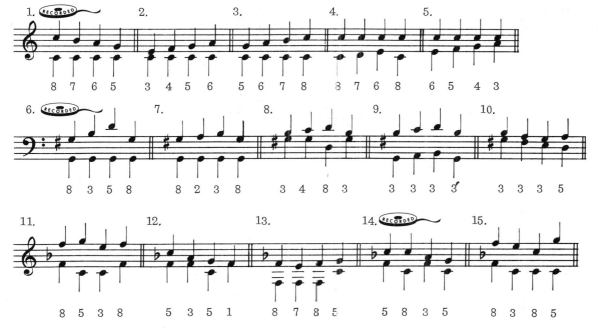

5 6 5 8   1 3 5 8   3 8 5 8   3 8 3 8   5 8 3 8

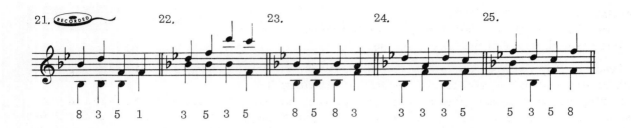

8 3 5 1   3 5 3 5   8 5 8 3   3 3 3 5   5 3 5 8

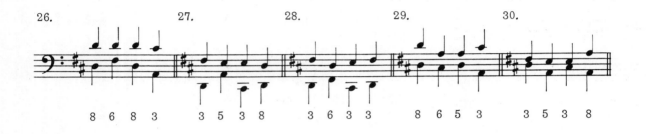

8 6 8 3   3 5 3 8   3 6 3 3   8 6 5 3   3 5 3 8

3 3 5 3   8 6 3 3   5 3 5 3   8 3 6 5   3 8 5 8

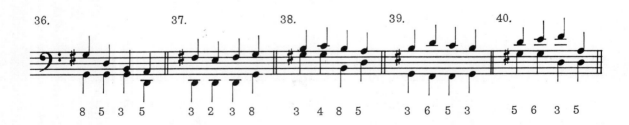

8 5 3 5   3 2 3 8   3 4 8 5   3 6 5 3   5 6 3 5

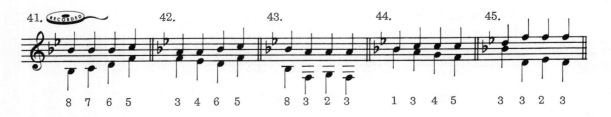

8 7 6 5   3 4 6 5   8 3 2 3   1 3 4 5   3 3 2 3

MELODY UNIT NO. 3

D. INTERVALS OF THE m 3, P 5, m 6, m 7

To the Student: The teacher will play an interval. The first note of the interval is given and is written on the staff for you.

Numbers 1 through 30—The given note is the *lower* note of the interval.

Numbers 31 through 60—The given note is the *upper* note of the interval.

Directions:
1. Write the name of the interval in the space provided.
2. Write the other note of the interval on the staff.

To the Teacher: Play the first note (whole note) then the second note (unstemmed black note). Have the students sing both notes immediately. Repeat the procedure if necessary.

Some teachers prefer to have the students associate each interval with a particular well known composition. The first two notes of "The More We Get Together" form the interval of a Perfect 5th. In the early stages of learning intervals this practice is effective, but later on instant recognition is seriously impaired—the procedure is too cumbersome.

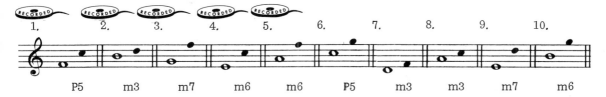

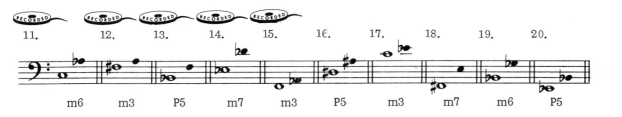

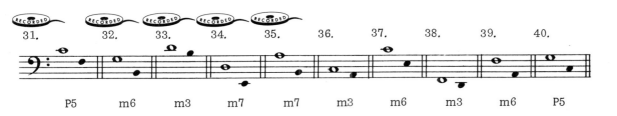

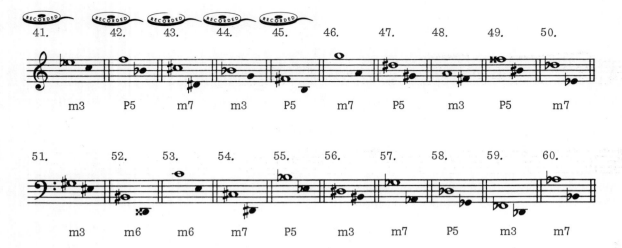

m3 P5 m7 m3 P5 m7 P5 m3 P5 m7

m3 m6 m6 m7 P5 m3 m7 P5 m3 m7

Workbook Page 20

MELODY UNIT NO. 4

A. DICTATION OF MELODIES EMPLOYING SCALEWISE PASSAGES AND ARPEGGIATIONS OF THE I AND V TRIADS

To the Student: In each exercise below you are given the key signature, the time signature and the first note only. You will hear a melodic phrase.

Directions: Complete the phrase on the staff in notation.

To the Teacher:
Procedure:
1. Have the students sing the scale of each exercise.
2. Play the exercise once or twice.
3. Have the students sing the exercise (from memory).
4. When the students can sing the exercise correctly, they are ready to write it on the staff.

The key signature, meter signature, and the first note of each exercise is given.

24. Chopin--Concerto

21

25. Brahms--Rhapsody

26. Beethoven--Symphony No. 6

27. Beethoven--Symphony No. 6

28. Mozart--Serenade in C Minor

MELODY UNIT NO. 4

Workbook Page 22

B. ERRORS IN THE DICTATION OF MELODY

To the Student: The melodies printed below are correct in every way. However, there are errors in the melodies as played by the instructor.

   Directions: Circle the notes that are not as played by the instructor.

To the Teacher: Play each melody exactly as written below. Have students sing the version as you play it and the version as it is written in the Student Workbook.

1.

2.

3.

"×" indicates notes which differ from those in Student Workbook.

22

4. Mozart--Serenade

5. Sibelius--Symphony No. 2

6.

7.

8. Haydn -- Symphony in D Major

MELODY UNIT NO. 4

Workbook Page 23

C. TWO VOICE EXERCISES

To the Student: Each exercise is in two voices.

Directions:

Numbers 1 through 22: Write the name of the interval formed (between the two voices) in the blanks below.

Numbers 23 through 53: Below are incompleted compositions in two voices. Add the missing notes on the staff in notation.

To the Teacher: These exercises are to lead up to the successful dictation of two voice exercises. Although the student will tend to hear each melody separately and will try to complete the dictation one voice at a time, it is more important that he hear the RELATIONSHIP of the two voices. Thus, the first 22 exercises require only the intervalic relationship of the two melodies. Beginning with Number 23 the student begins to write the actual notes of the melodies.

Dictate slowly enough to insure proper understanding. This may be as slow as two or three seconds per beat at the beginning. Try to increase the speed of dictation as the exercises progress.

The "X" is used in exercises, nos. 28-53 to indicate the notes the students must supply.

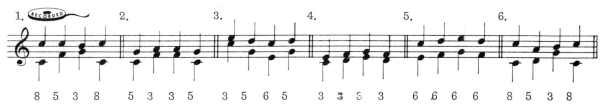

1.	2.	3.	4.	5.	6.
8 5 3 8	5 3 3 5	3 5 6 5	3 3 3 3	6 6 6 6	8 5 3 8

"×" indicates note missing in student workbook.

MELODY UNIT NO. 4
D. INTERVALS OF THE m 2, M 2, M 3, P 4, M 7, P 8

To the Student: The teacher will play an interval. The first note of the interval is given and is written on the staff for you.

Numbers 1 through 30—The given note is the *lower* note of the interval.

Numbers 31 through 60—The given note is the *upper* note of the interval.

Directions:
1. Write the name of the interval in the space provided.
2. Write the other note of the interval on the staff.

To the Teacher: Play the first note (whole note) then the second note (unstemmed black note). Have the students sing both notes immediately. Repeat the procedure if necessary.

MELODY UNIT NO. 5
A. MELODIES OUTLINING THE I, V, VII, AND IV TRIADS

To the Student: The teacher will play melodies outlining the I, V, VII, and IV triads.

Directions: Complete the compositions on the staff in notation.

To the Teacher: The first 12 exercises are less difficult and generally shorter than the succeeding 8. An above average class may skip many of the first 12 exercises and go directly to those taken from music literature. Less advantaged students should work all of the 12 exercises before approaching the more difficult set from 13 through 20.

Before dictating these exercises have the students sing the I, V, VII, and IV triads in various keys. Then, as each exercise is dictated have them sing these triads in the key of the composition.

Be sure each student can *sing* each exercise in its entirety before he writes it down.

The first note of each exercise is given in the Student Workbook.

13. Mozart—Fantasia in D Minor

14. Mozart—Concerto in C for Flute, Harp and Orchestra

15. Bach—Fugue No. 21

16. Beethoven—Sonata, Op. 79

17. Bach—Little Prelude

18. Schubert—Impromptu, Op. 90, No. 1

19. Haydn—String Quartet, Op. 76, No. 5

20. Beethoven—Sonata, Op. 57

28

20. Beethoven--Sonata, Op. 57

MELODY UNIT NO. 5

B. MELODIES INVOLVING LEAPS OUTLINING THE I, IV, AND V TRIADS

To the Student: The first note (occasionally others) of a melody is given. The entire melody will be played for you.

Directions: Complete the melody on the staff in notation.

To the Teacher: The first 20 melodies are generally shorter and easier than the following 8. Students who have difficulty with melodic dictation should concentrate on the easier melodies before going on to the longer and more difficult ones. Suggested procedure:
1. Have all students sing the scale of the melody.
2. Call out certain degrees of the scale and have the students sing these pitches.
3. Play the melody one or two times.
4. Before allowing the student to write the melody on score paper make sure he can sing it in its entirety.
5. The student then writes the melody on score paper.

Only first note of exercises 1-20 is given in Student Workbook.

In Exercises 21-28 the "×" indicates notes the student must supply.

26. D. Scarlatti--Sonata in D Major

27. Hayden--Symphony in G Major

28. Hayden--Symphony in D Major

MELODY UNIT NO. 5

Workbook Page 31

C. KEY FEELING AND MELODIC MEMORY

To the Student: The teacher plays a phrase of music. The only note given to you is the last note.

Directions:
Write:
1. Key Signature
2. Time Signature
3. The notes of the melody

To the Teacher: The first 12 exercises are short and quite simple. Some students will be able to bypass these and go on to the more difficult exercises, 13 through 20. Those who have difficulty should do the entire 16 preparatory exercises.

Procedure: Play the exercise once or twice. Then, have the students sing the scale in which they think the composition is written. Finally, have the students sing the melody itself. They are then ready to complete the key signature, the time signature, and the notes.

Should the students have difficulty determining the meter tap lightly the first beat of each measure (as indicated).

* "⊕" indicates notes supplied in the student workbook.

31

18. Hayden--Farewell Symphony

19. Hayden--Farewell Symphony

32

MELODY UNIT NO. 5
D. INTERVALS OF THE m 3, TRITONE (T), P 5, m 6, M 6, m 7

To the Student: The teacher will play an interval. The first note of the interval is given and is written on the staff for you.

Numbers 1 through 30—The given note is the *lower* note of the interval.

Numbers 31 through 60—The given note is the *upper* note of the interval.

Directions:
1. Write the name of the interval in the space provided.
2. Write the other note of the interval on the staff.

To the Teacher: Play the first note (whole note) then the second note (unstemmed black note). Have the students sing both notes immediately. Repeat the procedure if necessary.

MELODY UNIT NO. 6
A. ACCOMPANIED MELODY

To the Student: In each exercise below you are given the key signature, the time signature, and the first note only. You will hear a melodic phrase with a harmonic accompaniment.

Directions: Write the melody on the staff in notation.
Optional for advanced students: Indicate also the harmonic analysis of the chords used.

To the Teacher: This type of exercise is designed to enable students to distinguish melodies in a homophonic texture. The accompanying harmony has been kept simple for those teachers who lack facility on the piano. If the teacher desires he may elaborate on these harmonies to suit himself.
Only the first note of each exercise is given in Student Workbook.

1. RECORDED

2.

3. Handel--Sonata in G Minor

4. Handel--Fireworks Music

5. RECORDED

6. Couperin--Concerto No. 8 in G Major

7. Bach--Minuet from the Partita No. 3 for Violin alone

8. Bach--Bouree from the Partita No. 1 in B minor for Violin alone

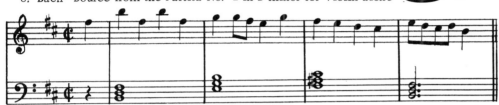

MELODY UNIT NO. 6

B. HARMONIC INTERVALS IN TWO VOICE WRITING

To the Student: The teacher will play a short phrase of music in two voices.

Directions: Write the numbers indicating the harmonic intervals occurring between the two voices. It is not necessary to give the quality of the interval. Thus, instead of P 8, M 3, A 4, M 7, etc., simply state 8, 3, 4, 7, etc.

To the Teacher: These exercises are designed to make the student more aware of the relationship between two melodies. In two part dictation, students, if left to their own devices, tend to ignore the harmonic relationships, and write each melody separately. This stress upon harmonic intervals provides a new dimension of relationship for the student, and directs his attention to the simultaneous sound of two concurrent melodies.

At first play the exercises slowly enough for the students to experience the harmonic intervals as separate entities. After some practice the students should be able to memorize both melodies by the harmonic intervals they create and write them down from memory. Little by little the tempo of dictation may be increased and the student will be able to memorize the sound of several intervals sounded in rapid succession.

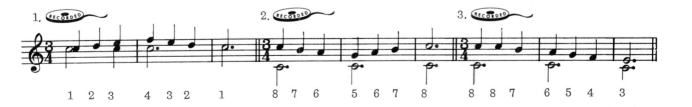

36

MELODY UNIT NO. 6
C. TWO PART DICTATION

To the Student: Each exercise is in two voices.

Directions:
Numbers 1 through 12: Write the name of the interval formed (harmonic intervals between the two voices) in the blanks below.
Numbers 13 through 34: Add the missing notes on the staff in notation.

To the Teacher: These exercises are to lead up to the successful dictation of two voice exercises. Although the student will tend to hear each melody separately and will try to complete the dictation one voice at a time, it is more important that he hear the RELATIONSHIP of the two voices. Thus, the first 12 exercises require only the intervalic relationship of the two melodies. Beginning with Number 13 the student begins to write the actual notes of the melodies.
Dictate slowly enough to insure proper understanding. This may be as slow as two or three seconds per beat at the beginning. Try to increase the speed of dictation as the exercises progress.

"×" indicates the note is missing in the student workbook.

MELODY UNIT NO. 6

D. INTERVALS OF THE m 6, M 6, m 7, M 7

To the Student: The teacher will play an interval. The first note of the interval is given and is written on the staff for you.

Numbers 1 through 30—The given note is the *lower* note of the interval.

Numbers 31 through 60—The given note is the *upper* note of the interval.

Directions:

1. Write the name of the interval in the space provided.
2. Write the other note of the interval on the staff.

To the Teacher: Play the first note (whole note) then the second note (unstemmed black note). Have the students sing both notes immediately. Repeat the procedure if necessary.

MELODY UNIT NO. 7

A. KEY FEELING AND MELODIC MEMORY

To the Student: The teacher plays a phrase of music. The only note given to you is the last note.

Directions:
Write:
1. Key Signature
2. Time Signature
3. The notes of the melody

To the Teacher: The first 16 exercises are short and quite simple. Some students will be able to bypass these and go on to the more difficult exercises, 17 through 24. Those who have difficulty should do the entire 16 preparatory exercises.

Procedure: Play the exercise once or twice. Then have the students sing the scale in which they think the composition is written. Finally, have the students sing the melody itself. They are then ready to complete the key signature, the time signature, and the notes.

In each exercise the last note only is given in the Student Workbook.

MELODY UNIT NO. 7

B. COMPARING MELODIES—SAME OR DIFFERENT

To the Student: You will hear two short melodies—one immediately following the other. Listen carefully for the PITCHES of each melody. Ignore rhythmic differences.

Directions: Place a line under SAME if the pitches of both melodies are the same. Disregard rhythm. Place a line under DIFFERENT if any of the pitches in the second melody are different from those of the first. Disregard rhythm.

To the Teacher: Play the first melody of each exercise and after a short pause play the second. A tempo of 100 per quarter note is suggested, but a slower or faster tempo may be taken at the discretion of the instructor.

1. Different

2. Different

3. Same

4. Same

5. Same

6. Different

7. Different

8.

Same

9.

Same

10.

Different

11.

Different

12.

Same

13.

Different

14.

Different

15.

Same

MELODY UNIT NO. 7

C. TWO VOICE COMPOSITIONS WITH ERRORS

To the Student: Below are a number of two voice compositions containing errors in pitch notation.

Directions: Place a circle around each note that does not conform to the version you hear.

To the Teacher: Play each exercise at a comfortable tempo. Exercises of this type can be played faster than those requiring the students to write out the notes.

"×"s indicate which notes should be circled by the student.

5. Bach--Little Prelude

6.

7. Bach--Little Fugue

8.

9.

10.

MELODY UNIT NO. 7

D. ALL INTERVALS

Workbook Page 43

To the Student: The teacher will play an interval. The first note of the interval is given and is written on the staff for you.

Numbers 1 through 30—The given note is the *lower* note of the interval.

Numbers 31 through 60—The given note is the *upper* note of the interval.

Directions:
1. Write the name of the interval in the space provided.
2. Write the other note of the interval on the staff.

To the Teacher: Play the first note (whole note) then the second note (unstemmed black note). Have the students sing both notes immediately. Repeat the procedure if necessary.

MELODY UNIT NO. 8

A. MELODIC DICTATION

To the Student: The first note only is given.

Directions:
1. Write the key signature.
2. Write the time signature.
3. Write the notes on the staff.

To the Teacher: Encourage the students to memorize the entire phrase before trying to write anything on paper.

Only the first note of each exercise is given in the student workbook.

47

MELODY UNIT NO. 8

B. MULTIPLE CHOICE

To the Student: The instructor will play three versions of each exercise. Only *one* is the same as that written.

Directions: Write "A," "B," or "C" in the blank provided. This will indicate which version played by the instructor is the same as that written below.

To the Teacher: Play each of the three possibilities at a normal speed and in a continuous fashion. These may be dictated faster than exercises involving the actual writing of notes on the staff.

1. a   Correct version

1. b

1. c

2. a   Romanian National Anthem

2. b

2. c   Correct version

3. a

3. b   Correct version

3. c

4. a

Correct version

4. b

4. c

5. a Chopin--Impromptu, Op. 36

5. b

Correct version

5. c

6. a Beethoven--Piano Sonata, Op. 7

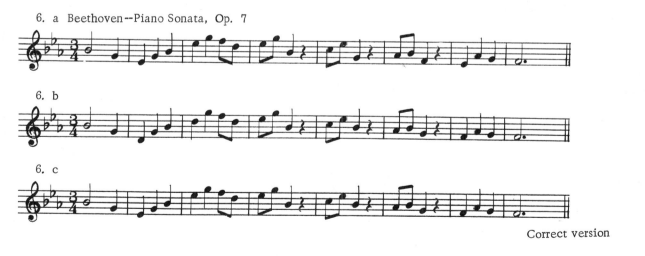

6. b

6. c

Correct version

7. a Beethoven--Piano Sonata, Op. 10, No. 2

7. b

Correct version

7. c

8. a Bach--Well Tempered Clavier, Book I, Fugue No. 21

8. b

Correct version

8. c

MELODY UNIT NO. 8

Workbook Page 47

C. TWO PART DICTATION

To the Student: Each exercise is a two voiced composition. The first note in each voice (and on occasion other notes) are given.

Directions: Add the missing notes on the staff in notation.

To the Teacher: Dictate slowly enough to insure proper understanding, but do not play either voice separately. Encourage the student to think in terms of the *harmonic* intervals which occur between the two voices. The teacher may establish a procedure of having the students name the harmonic intervals *before* writing the notes on the staff.

As the student increases his facility the teacher should increase the speed of dictation.

Exercises 1-6—First note in each voice is given in Student Workbook.
Exercises 7-18—"⊕" indicates note is given in Student Workbook.

1.   2.

50

MELODY UNIT NO. 8

Workbook Page 49

D. ALL INTERVALS

To the Student: The teacher will play an interval. The first note of the interval is given and is written on the staff for you.

Numbers 1 through 30—The given note is the *lower* note of the interval.

Numbers 31 through 60—The given note is the *upper* note of the interval.

Directions:
1. Write the name of the interval in the space provided.
2. Write the other note of the interval on the staff.

To the Teacher: Play the first note (whole note) then the second note (unstemmed black note). Have the students sing both notes immediately. Repeat the procedure if necessary.

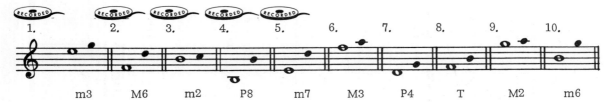

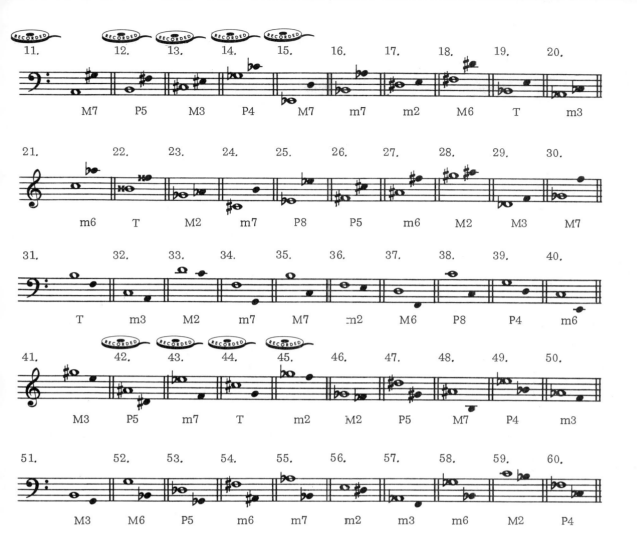

MELODY UNIT NO. 9

A. ACCOMPANIED MELODY

Workbook Page 50

To the Student: You are given the key signature, the time signature, and the first note of each exercise. You will hear a melodic phrase with a harmonic accompaniment.

Directions: Write the notes of the melody on the staff.
Optional: In addition write a harmonic analysis of the accompaniment.

To the Teacher: This type of exercise is designed to enable students to distinguish melodies in a homophonic texture. The accompanying harmony has been kept simple for those teachers who lack facility on the piano. If the teacher desires he may elaborate on these harmonies to suit himself. If the student is unable to comprehend the larger units, it may be wise to break these exercises into smaller sections of two or three measures.

The first note and other notes marked "⊕" are given in the Student Workbook.

2. Hayden--Quartet in F Op. 3, No. 5

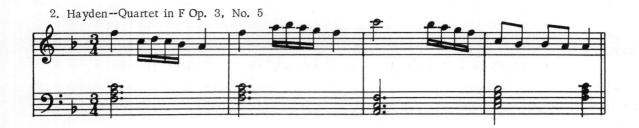

3. Sammartini--Canto Amoroso (Violin & Piano)

4. Rimsky-Korsakoff--Snow Maiden

5. Rossini--Barber of Seville

6. Rossini--William Tell

MELODY UNIT NO. 9
B. INTERVALS FORMED BY TWO MELODIC LINES

To the Student: Each exercise below consists of *four* harmonic intervals. These will be played slowly in succession by the teacher. Listen carefully to each interval formed.

Directions:
Numbers 1 through 20:

Write the name of the interval formed in the blanks below. It is not necessary to name the *quality* of the interval—only the interval itself.

For example, in the first exercise the teacher plays:

You write in the blanks: 3   4   3   5

Numbers 21 through 40:

Same as for Numbers 1 through 20 except that you are now asked to name the *quality* of the interval as well as the number representing it. Your answer for number 21 should be: P4, P5, P4, P5.

To the Teacher: Play each interval at the rate of about one per second, slower if necessary. As the students become more proficient at recognizing intervals quickly, ask them to relate the answers verbally.

55

21.   22.   23.   24.   25.

P4 P5 P4 P5   P4 P4 P4 P5   P5 m7 P5 m6   M3 P4 M3 P5   P4 P5 P4 P5

26.   27.   28.   29.   30.

m3 m6 m3 P5   P4 P5 P4 P5   P5 P4 P4 P5   m3 M6 M6 M3   P5 P5 P5 P5

31.   32.   33.   34.   35.

T T T T   m7 M2 m7 M2   M7 m7 T m7   M3 m6 M3 M6   m2 P5 m7 P5

36.   37.   38.   39.   40.

M7 T M2 M7   m7 M7 P4 T   m7 M7 M7 P8   T m7 T m7   m7 T m7 M7

MELODY UNIT NO. 9

Workbook Page 52

C. TWO VOICE DICTATION

To the Student: The teacher will play a short phrase of music in two voices.

Directions:
Numbers 1 through 10: Write the numbers indicating the harmonic intervals occurring between the two voices. It is not necessary to give the quality of the interval. Thus, instead of P 8, M 3, A 4, M 7, etc. simply state 8, 3, 4, 7, etc.

Numbers 11 through 16: Complete the two voice compositions as dictated.

To the Teacher: The first 10 exercises are designed to make the student more aware of the relationship between two melodies. At first play the exercises slowly enough for the students to experience the harmonic intervals as separate entities. Little by little the tempo of dictation may be increased and the student will be able to memorize the sound of several intervals sounded in rapid succession.

For the exercises from 11 through 16 dictate both voices at the same time trying to give equal emphasis to each voice.

"⊕" indicates note is provided in student workbook.

MELODY UNIT NO. 9

D. THE HARMONIC INTERVALS OF THE P 8, P 4, M 7, M 2, m 2, M 3

To the Student: The teacher will play an interval (harmonic interval). The first note of the interval is given and is written on the staff for you.

Numbers 1 through 30—The given note is the *lower* note of the interval.

Numbers 31 through 60—The given note is the *upper* note of the interval.

Directions:
1. Write the name of the interval in the space provided.
2. Write the other note of the interval on the staff.

To the Teacher: Play both notes of the interval simultaneously. Have the students sing the notes immediately. Repeat the procedure if necessary.

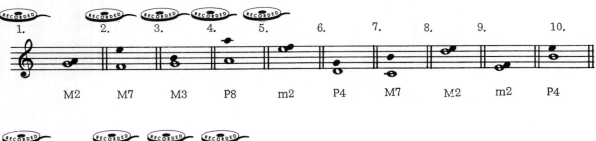

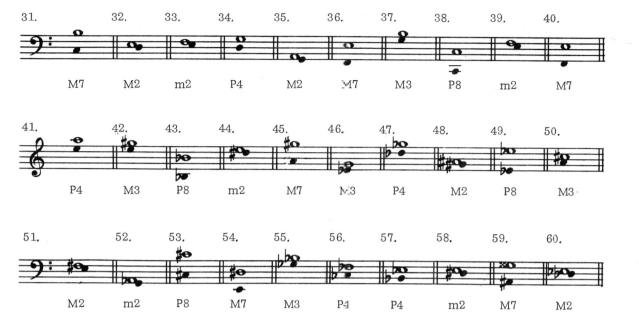

31.	32.	33.	34.	35.	36.	37.	38.	39.	40.
M7	M2	m2	P4	M2	M7	M3	P8	m2	M7

41.	42.	43.	44.	45.	46.	47.	48.	49.	50.
P4	M3	P8	m2	M7	M3	P4	M2	P8	M3

51.	52.	53.	54.	55.	56.	57.	58.	59.	60.
M2	m2	P8	M7	M3	P4	P4	m2	M7	M2

MELODY UNIT NO. 10

A. RECOGNITION OF PHRASE RELATIONSHIPS

To the Student: Each exercise consists of two four-measure phrases related in one of the following ways:
REPEATED PHRASES: Measures 1 2 3 4 are the same as 5 6 7 8

PARALLEL PHRASES: Measures 1 2 are same as 5 6
    Measures 3 4 are different from 7 8

CONTRASTING PHRASES: Measures 1 2 3 4 are different from 5 6 7 8

Directions:
1. Mark REPEATED in the blank if measures 1 2 3 4 are the same as 5 6 7 8.
2. Mark PARALLEL in the blank if measures 1 2 are same as 5 6, but 3 4 are different from 7 8.
3. Mark CONTRASTING in the blank if measures 1 2 3 4 are different from 5 6 7 8.

To the Teacher:
1. Play the examples shown above for the students
2. Then, play the exercises at about MM 60 per dotted half note.

MELODY UNIT NO. 10

B. NON-MODULATING AND MODULATING MELODIES

To the Student: The teacher will play a melody for you. The first note of each melody is given.

Numbers 1 through 11—These melodies do not modulate.

Numbers 12 through 19—These melodies modulate.

Directions: Complete the melody (as dictated) on the staff.

To the Teacher: In presenting the melodies, 12 through 19, have the students sing the tonic at the beginning of the composition. Then, play the melody. Have the students sing the new tonic. Make sure they hear and understand the interval relationship between the two tonics. Then, they are ready to take the melodies from dictation.

The first note and others marked "⊕" are given in the Student Workbook.

MELODY UNIT NO. 10
C. NON-MODULATING MELODIES FROM LITERATURE

To the Student: The teacher will play a melody for you. The first note of each melody is given.

Directions: Complete the melody (as dictated) on the staff.

To the Teacher: Before dictating each exercise have the students sing the scale of the composition. Then, call out random degrees of the scale and have the students sing these degrees as they are called. When the students are properly oriented dictate the melody.

The first note of each exercise and additional notes marked "⊕" are given in the Student Workbook.

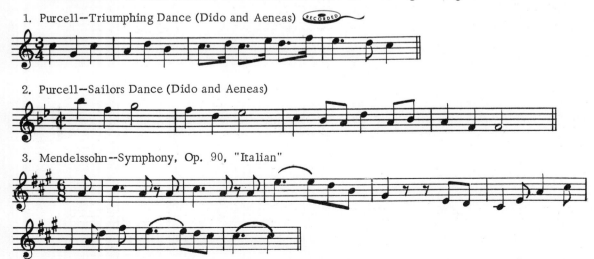

1. Purcell—Triumphing Dance (Dido and Aeneas) RECORDED

2. Purcell—Sailors Dance (Dido and Aeneas)

3. Mendelssohn—Symphony, Op. 90, "Italian"

4. Brahms--Waltzes, Op. 39

5. Beethoven--Sonata, Op. 90

6.

Workbook Page 58

MELODY UNIT NO. 10

D. HARMONIC INTERVALS OF THE m 3, TRITONE, P 5, m 6, M 6, m 7

To the Student: The teacher will play an interval (harmonic interval). The first note of the interval is given and is written on the staff for you.

Numbers 1 through 30—The given note is the *lower* note of the interval.

Numbers 31 through 60—The given note is the *upper* note of the interval.

Directions:

1. Write the name of the interval in the space provided.
2. Write the other note of the interval on the staff.

To the Teacher: Play both notes of the interval simultaneously. Have the students sing the notes immediately. Repeat the procedure if necessary.

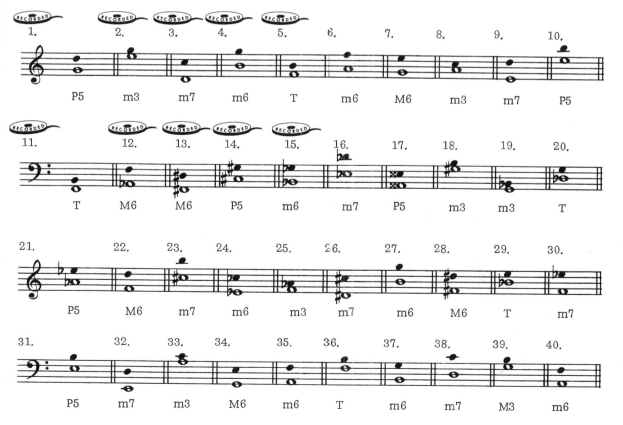

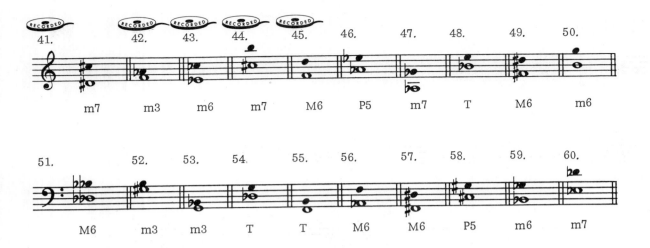

MELODY UNIT NO. 10

Workbook Page 59

E. MELODIC SEQUENCES

To the Student: The teacher will play a four-note melody and follow it with an additional four notes—a sequential pattern of the same melody.

Sequence—The repetition (in the same melodic line) of a short musical phrase at another pitch.

Diatonic Sequence—The pitches of the sequence adhere strictly to the notes of the diatonic scale.

Non-diatonic Sequence—The pitches of the sequence do not adhere to the notes of the diatonic scale, but may either modulate to another key or follow a chromatic pattern.

Directions: Complete the melody by adding the remaining four notes on the staff in notation.

To the Teacher:

1. Play the melody of 8 notes.
2. Have the students immediately sing what you have played.
3. Students may then complete the notation.

A speed of about 100 per whole note is suggested. You may wish to pause slightly after the first group of four notes.

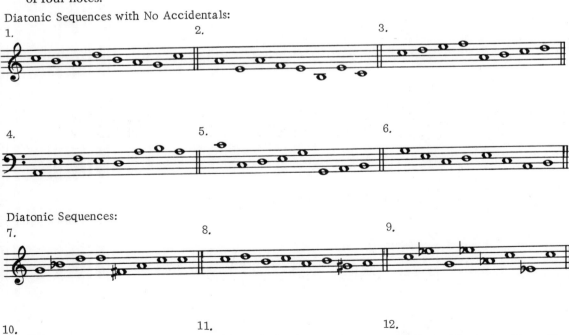

Non-Diatonic Sequences:

13.   14.   15.

16.   17.   18.

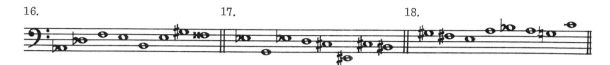

19.   20.   21.

MELODY UNIT NO. 11

Workbook Page 61

A. MELODIC DICTATION

To the Student: The first note only is given.

Directions:
1. Write the key signature.
2. Write the time signature.
3. Write the notes on the staff.

To the Teacher: Encourage the students to memorize the entire phrase before trying to write anything on paper. In each exercise the first note only is given.

1. Franck--Quintet in F Minor (RECORDED)

2. Farnaby--Tower Hill (From the Fitzwilliam Virginal Book)

3. Corelli--Sonata Da Camera, Op. 2, No. 5

4. Corelli--Concerto Grosso, Op. 6, No. 11

5. Mozart--Eine Kleine Nachtmusik (RECORDED)

6. Mozart--Eine Kleine Nachtmusik (RECORDED)

MELODY UNIT NO. 11
B. MELODIES WHICH MODULATE TO CLOSELY RELATED KEYS

To the Student: Each of the following melodies modulates to a closely related key. The teacher will play the exercise slowly for you.

Directions: Write the melody on the staff in notation.

To the Teacher: Play each melody once or twice. Have the students first sing the tonic which prevails at the beginning of the melody and the tonic which prevails at the end. After the relationship of tonics is well in mind, have the students then complete the writing of the melody on score paper.

The first note of each exercise and other notes marked "⊕" are given in the Student Workbook.

Workbook Page 63

MELODY UNIT NO. 11

C. TWO VOICE DICTATION

To the Student: The teacher will play a short phrase of music in two voices.

Directions:

Numbers 1 through 10: Write the numbers indicating the harmonic intervals occurring between the two voices. It is not necessary to give the quality of the interval. Thus, instead of P 8, M 3, A 4, M 7, etc. simply state 8, 3, 4, 7, etc.

Numbers 11 through 16: Complete the two voice compositions as dictated. The first note in each voice is given.

To the Teacher: The first 10 exercises are designed to make the student more aware of the relationship between two melodies. At first play the exercises slowly enough for the students to experience the harmonic intervals as separate entities. Little by little the tempo of dictation may be increased and the student will be able to memorize the sound of several intervals sounded in rapid succession.

For the exercises from 11 through 16 dictate both voices at the same time trying to give equal emphasis to each voice.

⊕ indicates note (or rest) is provided in student workbook.

16.

MELODY UNIT NO. 11

Workbook Page 65

D. ALL INTERVALS PLAYED HARMONICALLY

To the Student: The teacher will play an interval (harmonic interval). The first note of the interval is given and is written on the staff for you.

Numbers 1 through 30—The given note is the *lower* note of the interval.
Numbers 31 through 60—The given note is the *upper* note of the interval.

Directions:
1. Write the name of the interval in the space provided.
2. Write the other note of the interval on the staff.

To the Teacher: Play both notes of the interval simultaneously. Have the students sing the notes immediately. Repeat the procedure if necessary, then have the students complete the directions above.

1.	2.	3.	4.	5.	6.	7.	8.	9.	10.
m7	P4	M3	m2	M6	P8	m3	M2	M7	m6

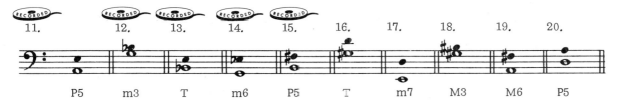

11.	12.	13.	14.	15.	16.	17.	18.	19.	20.
P5	m3	T	m6	P5	T	m7	M3	M6	P5

21.	22.	23.	24.	25.	26.	27.	28.	29.	30.
P4	M3	M2	m6	m2	M7	P8	m2	m3	P5

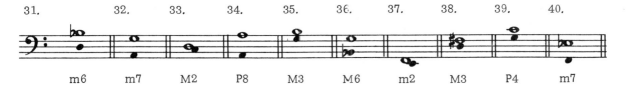

31.	32.	33.	34.	35.	36.	37.	38.	39.	40.
m6	m7	M2	P8	M3	M6	m2	M3	P4	m7

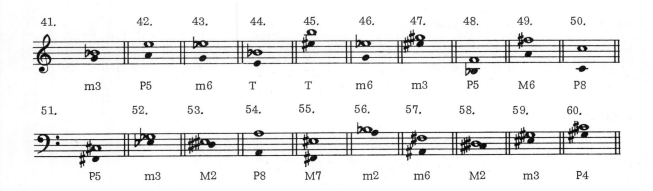

MELODY UNIT NO. 12

A. SIMPLE MODULATIONS TO CLOSELY RELATED KEYS

To the Student: Each exercise is a melodic phrase. The meter signature, key signature, and first note of each is given.

Directions: Write the remainder of the melody on the staff in notation.

To the Teacher: Have the students sing each melody before writing it on paper.
The beginning note and others marked ⊕ are provided in the stuednt workbook.

7 Cimarosa--11 Matrimonio Segreto (Overture)

8. Chopin--Etude, Op. 25, No. 5

MELODY UNIT NO. 12

Workbook Page 67

B. ACCIDENTALS

To the Student: Each exercise is a melodic phrase. All notes are correct except that they lack proper accidentals.

Directions: Add the accidentals to make the pitches conform to those played by the instructor.

To the Teacher: Play the exercise once or twice. Have the students sing it as *played*, then as *written*. When the difference is clear the students should then add the accidentals on paper.

1. Chopin--Mazurka, Op. 41, No. 2 (RECORDED)

2. Chopin--Mazurka, Op. 67, No. 3

3. Bach--Organ Fugue No. 12 in G Minor (RECORDED)

4. Bach--Theme for Musical Offering (RECORDED)

5.

6.

MELODY UNIT NO. 12
C. MORE DIFFICULT TWO VOICE COMPOSITIONS

To the Student: Each exercise is an incompleted composition in two voices.

Directions: Add the missing notes to the staff in notation.

To the Teacher: Play the two voices as written. Playing either voice separately defeats the purpose of this drill.

The beginning note and others marked "⊕" are provided in the student workbook.

5. Palestrina--Motet, O Quantus Luctus (Invertible at the Octave)

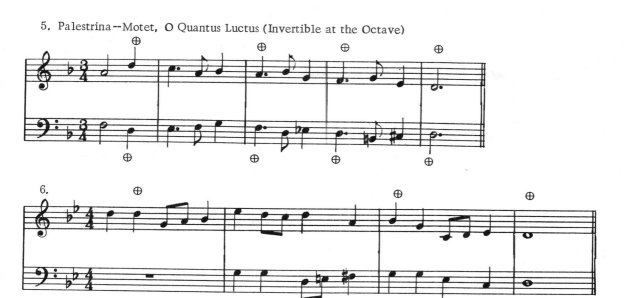

MELODY UNIT NO. 12

D. INTERVALS

To the Student: The first three notes of each exercise are given. An additional three notes are missing.

Directions: Write the missing notes on the staff.

To the Teacher: Exercises of this type are designed to drill the students in melodies of a more contemporary nature (less tonally oriented). These are to be read as single measures of normal printed music. If an accidental occurs beside a tone early in the series it is intended that this accidental will carry through the group of six. In some instances the accidentals have been added throughout the group simply to facilitate reading.

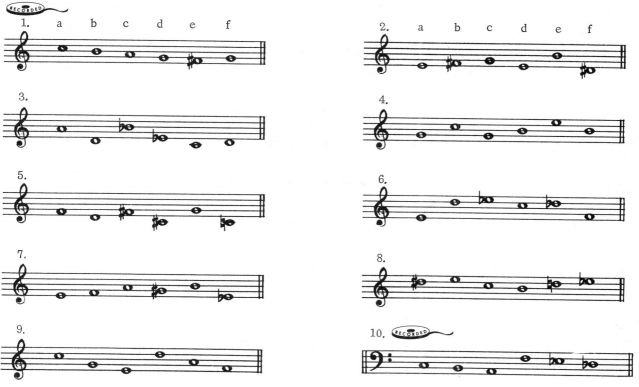

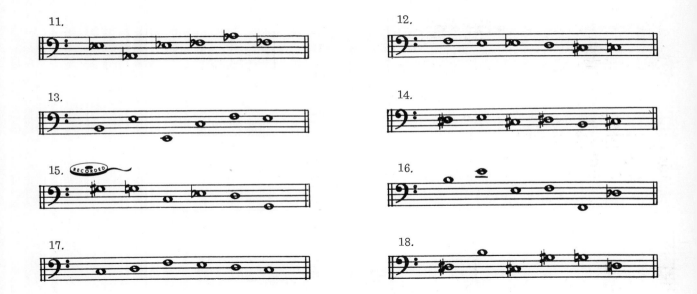

MELODY UNIT NO. 13

Workbook Page 71

A. MODAL MELODIES

To the Student: Each exercise employs a church mode. In all exercises except No. 11 the first and last note is the same, and in *all* exercises the last note is the "final" or first degree of the mode (corresponding to "tonic" in tonal systems). Modes you may hear are:

1. Dorian—(D to D on white keys of the piano) sounds like the natural minor scale with a raised sixth degree.
2. Phrygian—(E to E on white keys of the piano) sounds like the natural minor scale with a lowered second degree.
3. Lydian—(F to F on white keys of the piano) sounds like a major scale with a raised fourth degree.
4. Mixolydian—(G to G on white keys of the piano) sounds like the major scale with a lowered seventh degree.
5. Aeolian—(A to A on white keys of the piano) this *is* the natural minor scale.
6. Ionian—(C to C on white keys of the piano) this *is* the major scale.

Directions: Write the name of the mode in the blank.

To the Teacher: Play the exercise once or twice. Have the students sing the mode (using the last note of the exercise to begin on) as a scale. Determine the mode (by comparisons with major and natural minor scales).

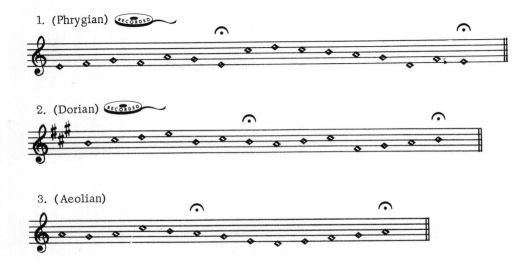

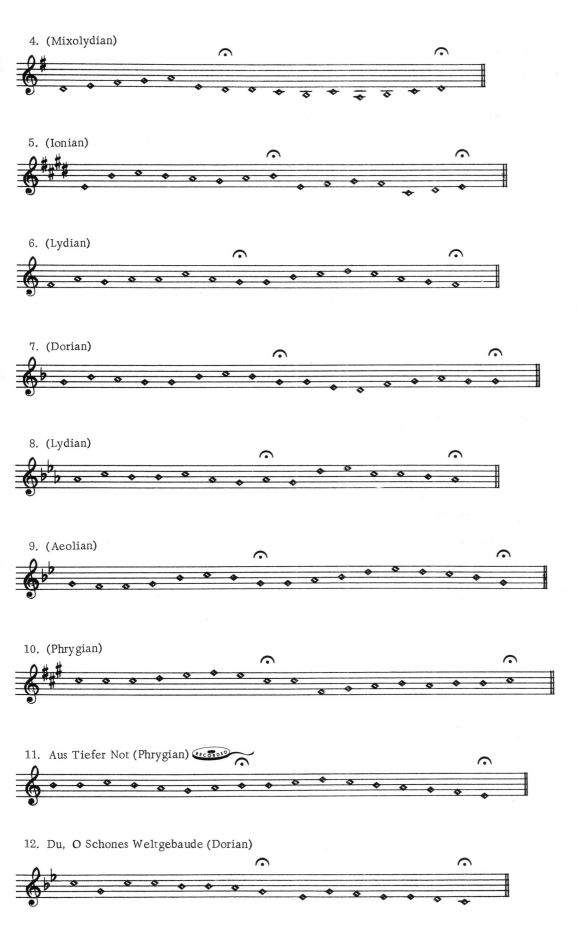

MELODY UNIT NO. 13
B. MODAL DICTATION

To the Student: Each of the following exercises is in one of the church modes. You are given the signature and the first note of the melody.

    Directions: Write the melody on the staff. Disregard rhythm. Write all notes black and unstemmed (as shown).

To the Teacher: Rhythm has been omitted from the following exercises. Dictate by phrase, and have students sing each phrase correctly (after hearing) before writing it on paper.
    The first note of each exercise is given.

1. Allein Zu Dir, Herr Jesu Christ (Lutheran Chorale) (Aeolian)

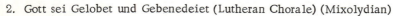

2. Gott sei Gelobet und Gebenedeiet (Lutheran Chorale) (Mixolydian)

3. Nun freut Euch, Gottes Kinder All' (Lutheran Chorale) (Dorian)

4. Ach Gott, Vom Himmel Sieh' Darein (Lutheran Chorale) (Phrygian)

5. (Lydian)

6. (Mixolydian)

76

MELODY UNIT NO. 13
C. TWO VOICE MODAL COMPOSITIONS

To the Student: The following exercises are similar to previous two voice compositions except that they are chosen from the style of the two voice counterpoint of the 16th century.

Directions: Complete the melodies on the staff in music notation.

To the Teacher: Give the students an opportunity to sing the missing notes after you have played the exercise once or twice. Then, they may write them on the staff.

1. Palestrina -- Mass, Ecce Sacerdos Magnus (Credo)

2. Palestrina -- Mass, Ecce Sacerdos Magnus (Credo)

3. Palestrina -- Mass, Gabriel Archangelus (Credo)

4. Palestrina -- Mass, Gabriel Archangelus (Sanctus)

---

*"×" indicates notes missing in the Student Workbook.

5. Palestrina -- Mass, Gabriel Archangelus (Sanctus)

6. Palestrina -- Mass, Gabriel Archangelus (Agnus Dei)

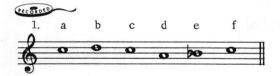

Workbook Page 73

MELODY UNIT NO. 13
D. INTERVALS IN MODAL PATTERNS

To the Student: The first three notes of a six note melody are given.

Directions: Write the remaining three notes on the staff in notation. Use whole notes (as shown).

To the Teacher: Play the exercise once or twice. Have the students sing all six notes accurately before writing them on paper.

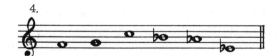

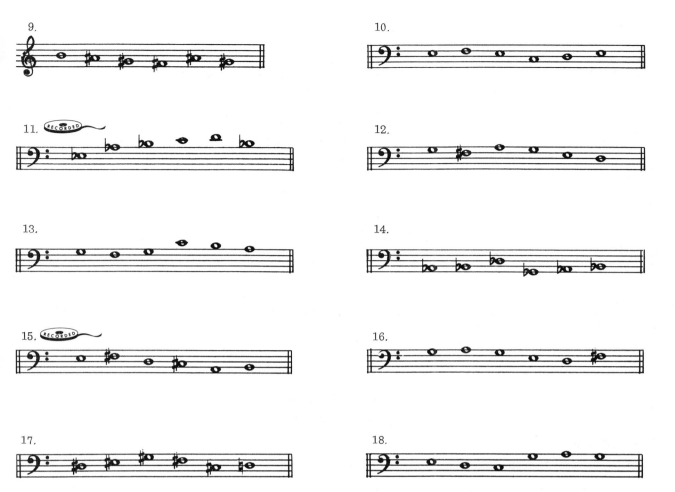

MELODY UNIT NO. 14

A. MELODIC DICTATION

To the Student: In the exercises below you are given the first note and occasionally other notes.

Directions: Complete the exercises on the staff in notation.

To the Teacher:
1. Play the first phrase twice.
2. Play the first phrase and add the second phrase.
3. Play the second phrase again.
4. Play the second phrase and add the third phrase.
5. Continue in this fashion until all phrases have been played.
This section is designed to teach phrase connection. Only exercise No. 1 is a single phrase—here the student should distinguish the sequence as an aid in dictation.
Notes marked "⊕" are given in Student Workbook.

1. LeClair, Trio Sonata, Op. 2, No. 8

2.

3.

4. Mozart--Symphony in G Minor, K 550 (Minuet) RECORDED

5. Mozart--Symphony in C Major, K 551 "Jupiter" (Minuet)

6. Haydn--Symphony in E Flat (Fourth Movement, Vivace)

80

MELODY UNIT NO. 14
B. MODAL DICTATION

To the Student: Each of the following exercises is in one of the church modes. You are given the signature and the first note of the melody.

Directions: Complete the exercise on the staff. Use unstemmed quarter notes. Disregard rhythm.

To the Teacher: Rhythm has been omitted from the following exercises. Dictate by phrase. Have students sing each phrase (immediately after you play it) before writing it down.

The first note of each exercise is given in the student workbook.

1. Meine Seel' Erhebt Den Herren (Lutheran Chorale) (Aeolian)

2. (Mixolydian)

3. (Ionian)

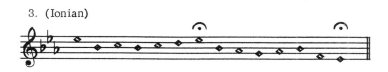

4. (Dorian)

5. (Dorian)

6. (Lydian)

MELODY UNIT NO. 14
C. TWO VOICE MODAL COMPOSITION

To the Student: The following exercises are chosen from the style of contrapuntal writing peculiar to the 16th century.

Directions: Complete the melodies on the staff in notation.

To the Teacher: Play the two melodies balanced, so that neither stands out separately.

1. Palestrina--Canon from Mass, Ad Coenam Agni Providi

2. Palestrina--Benedictus from Mass, Ad Coenam Agni Providi

3. Palestrina--Benedictus from Mass, Pro Defunctis

4.

*"×" indicates notes missing in the Student Workbook.

5. Orlando Di Lasso--Canons in Two Voices

6. Orlando Di Lasso--Benedictus

Workbook Page 78

MELODY UNIT NO. 14

D. RECOGNITION OF VARIOUS SCALE FORMATIONS

To the Student: Each exercise is an 8 measure melody employing *one* of the following scales or systems:

PENTATONIC

DIATONIC MAJOR

DIATONIC MINOR

DORIAN MODE

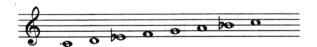

GYPSY MINOR

WHOLE TONE

CHROMATIC Employs all twelve tones. The examples in this section are key oriented.

ATONAL Employs all twelve tones and avoids a key center.

Directions: Name the type of scale or system used in each exercise.
Optional for advanced students: Write the entire composition on the staff in notation.

To the Teacher:
1. Play over each scale above and discuss.
2. Play the exercise once or twice at about 60 MM per dotted half note.
3. If you play this for advanced students to complete on the staff, a slower speed will be necessary. The first note of each exercise is given in Student Workbook.

7. ATONAL

8. WHOLE TONE

9. GYPSY MINOR

10. CHROMATIC

11. DIATONIC MINOR

MELODY UNIT NO. 15

Workbook Page 81

A. MELODIC DICTATION

To the Student: In the exercises below you are given the first note of the phrase and an occasional note throughout the composition.

    Directions: Complete each composition on the staff in notation.

To the Teacher:
1. Play each phrase two times.
2. Play the phrase a third time and this time connect it with the next phrase.
Notes marked "⊕" are given in Student Workbook.

1.

2. Beethoven--Sonata, Op. 10, No. 3 (Minuet)

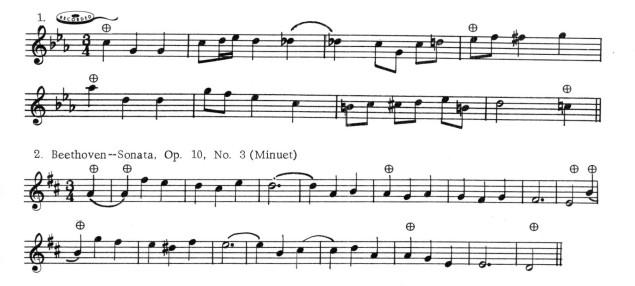

MELODY UNIT NO. 15

Workbook Page 82

B. ACCOMPANIED MELODY

To the Student: You will hear a melody with a background accompaniment.

Directions:
1. Write the notes of the melody on the staff.
2. Write the letter name of the "chord" root in the blank.
3. Write the coloration (Major, Minor, Diminished, Augmented) in the blank after the letter name.

To the Teacher: This type of exercise is designed to enable the student to separate melody in a homophonic structure, and to identify the nature of the accompanying harmonic structure. Do not insist on a Roman Numeral analysis of the chords as yet, but allow the student to give the letter names of the chords and their colorations (Major, Minor, Diminished, Augmented, and Major-minor sevenths).

The first note of each exercise is given in the Student Workbook.

1. Buxtehude--Sarabande

2. Buxtehude--Aria

3. Schubert--Valses Nobles, Op. 77, No. 10

4.

5.

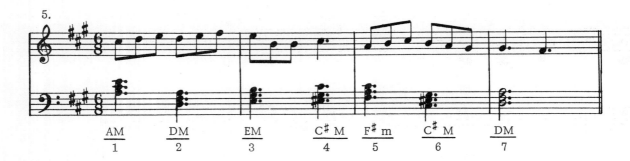

AM 1 | DM 2 | EM 3 | C#M 4 | F#m 5 | C#M 6 | DM 7

6.

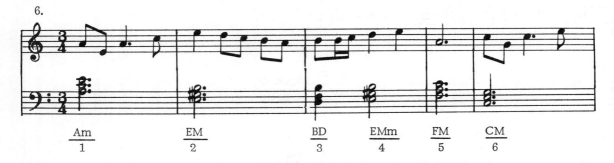

Am 1 | EM 2 | BD 3 | EMm 4 | FM 5 | CM 6

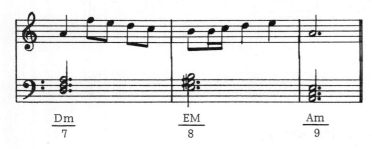

Dm 7 | EM 8 | Am 9

MELODY UNIT NO. 15

Workbook Page 83

C. HARMONIC INTERVALS

To the Student: The first three (of a set of six) intervals are given.

    Directions: Write the remaining intervals on the staff in notation.

To the Teacher: Play the exercise once or twice. Have the students immediately name the quality of all intervals. Then, they may write the notes on the staff.

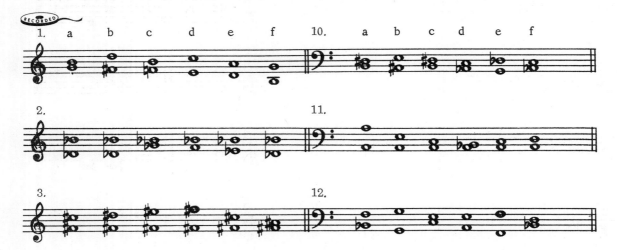

Workbook Page 84

MELODY UNIT NO. 15
D. MORE DIFFICULT MELODIC INTERVALS

To the Student: The first three notes of a seven note melody are given.

Directions: Complete the remaining four notes on the staff.

To the Teacher: Play the melody of seven notes. Have the students immediately sing these back to you. When they can sing all the notes accurately, then they should write them on paper.

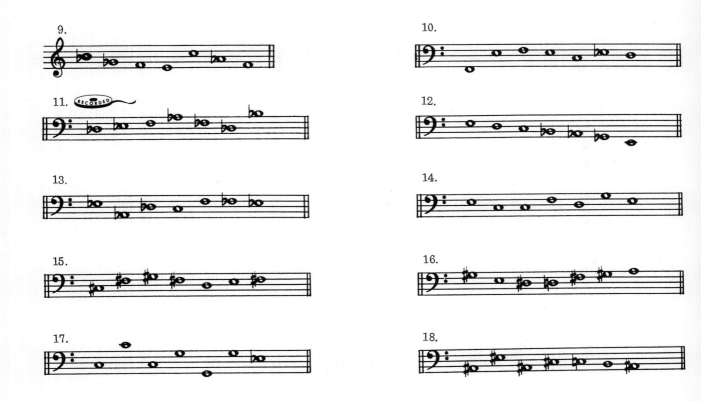

MELODY UNIT NO. 16

A. MELODIC DICTATION

To the Student: You are given the first note of the phrase and an occasional note throughout the melody.

Directions: Complete the melody on the staff.

To the Teacher: This is another set of exercises which entails the connecting of two or more phrases. Play each phrase two times, and the connection between the phrases once.
Notes marked "⊕" are given in Student Workbook.

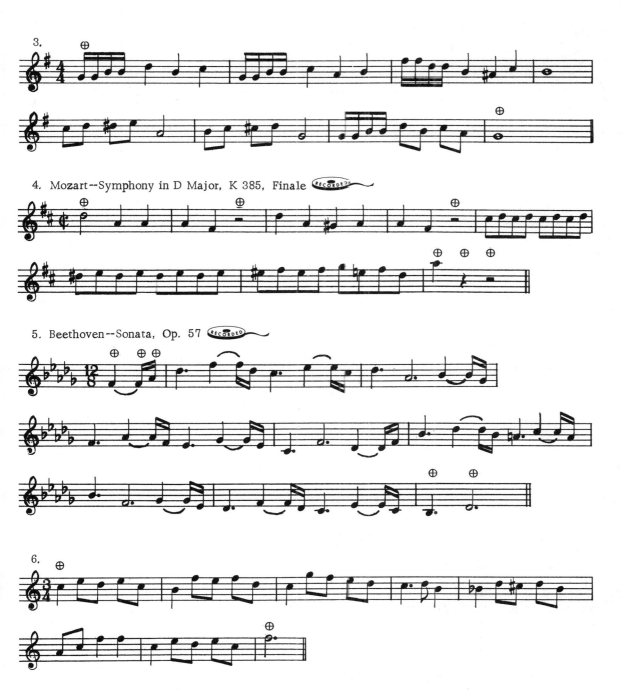

3.

4. Mozart--Symphony in D Major, K 385, Finale

5. Beethoven--Sonata, Op. 57

6.

Workbook Page 87

MELODY UNIT NO. 16

B. ACCOMPANIED MELODY

To the Student: Each exercise is a melody with background accompaniment.

Directions:
1. Write the melody on the staff in notation.
2. Write the letter name of the root in the blank.
3. Write the coloration (Major, Minor, Diminished, etc.) in the blank after the letter name of the root.

To the Teacher: Most of these exercises will require dictation by phrase. Dictate the first phrase twice, then play it a third time adding the second phrase, and so on. If students have difficulty with the background accompaniment, have them sing the notes of each chord as it is played.

The first note of each exercise is given in the student workbook.

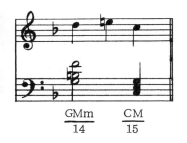

GMm   CM
14   15

4.

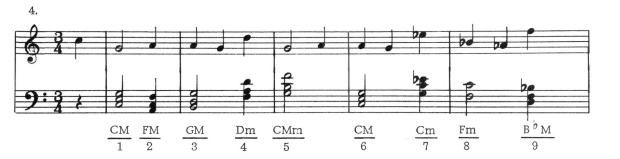

CM FM   GM   Dm CMm   CM   Cm   Fm   B♭M
1   2   3   4   5   6   7   8   9

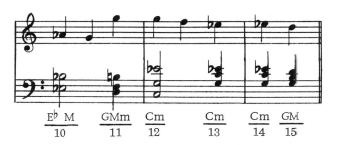

E♭M   GMm Cm   Cm   Cm GM
10   11   12   13   14 15

5. Purcell--Trumpet call

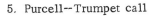

CM   CM   GM   CM   CM   GM
1   2   3   4   5   6

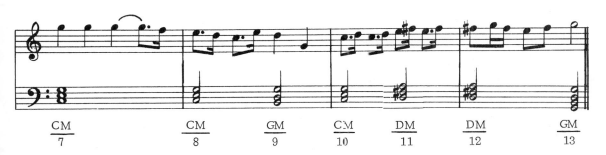

CM   CM   GM   CM   DM   DM   GM
7   8   9   10   11   12   13

6.

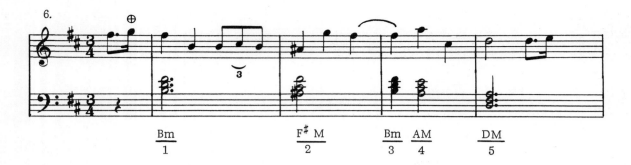

Bm
1

F#M
2

Bm AM
3 4

DM
5

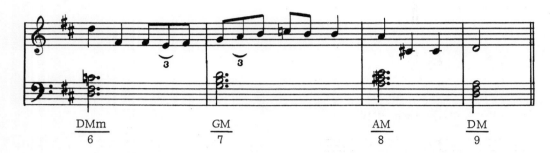

DMm
6

GM
7

AM
8

DM
9

MELODY UNIT NO. 16

Workbook Page 89

C. TWO VOICE COMPOSITIONS

To the Student: The following exercises are chosen from various styles of two voice writing.

   Directions: Complete the two voices on the staff in notation.

To the Teacher: Play each composition slowly and deliberately with equal stress on the two voices. "⊕" indicates notes given in Student Workbook.

1. Bach--Aria

2. Buxtehude--Sarabande

3.

4. Palestrina--Mass, Gabriel Archangelus (Benedictus)

5. Clementi--Sonata, Op. 36, No. 5 (RECORDED)

6. Haydn--Andante Grazioso

MELODY UNIT NO. 16
D. SEQUENCE PATTERNS IN MELODIC INTERVALS

To the Student: The first three notes of an eight note melody are given. Many of the exercises contain sequences. Listen carefully for these. The sequence leg may be of two, three, or four notes.

Directions:
1. Write the remaining five notes on the staff.
2. Bracket the sequence legs.

To the Teacher: These exercises deal with sequences of melodic pitch. Sometimes the sequence leg is of two notes repeated three times, three notes repeated once (with two notes left over), or four notes repeated once.
Play the melody once or twice. Have the students immediately sing back the melody and describe the nature of the sequence, i.e. how many notes, how far apart, etc. After the melody pattern is thoroughly understood the students may then write the notes on the paper.

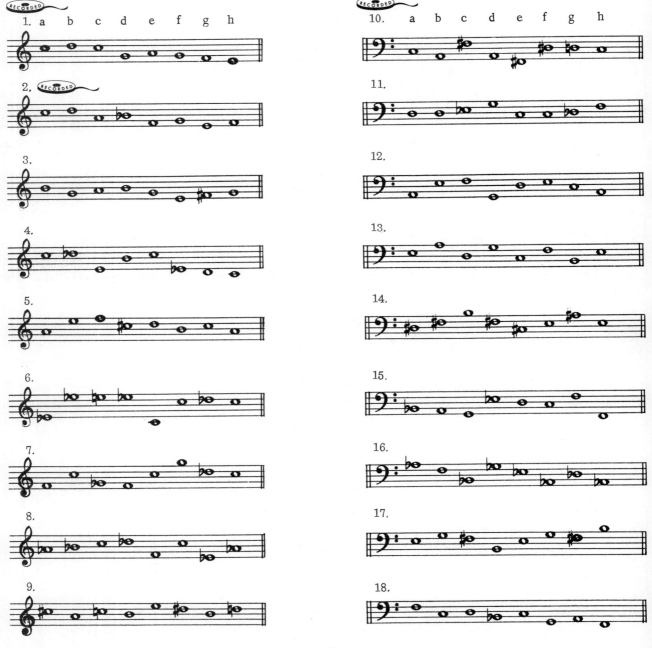

INTRODUCTION

HARMONY UNITS

Since harmony is but another aspect or approach to music it may be safely assumed that harmonic dictation may be taken up simultaneously with melodic dictation. In the introduction to the Melody Units it was suggested that scale drills be instituted at the very beginning of the course. These would lead naturally of course to melodic patterns within the scale. The same procedure is to be followed in harmony with the class drills leading directly into meaningful harmonic patterns. These harmonic drills should be taken up along with the scale drills which are explained in the section of this book entitled "Melody Units."

SUGGESTED CLASS DRILLS IN HARMONY

1. Introduce immediately the triad. Students should learn to sing triads on any given pitch (within their vocal range).

   a. At first students sing major triads beginning with the root.

   Instructor plays:

   Student then sings (using triad factor numbers):

   As soon as this is digested and the student can sing a major triad with a fair degree of accuracy the minor triad should be taken up.

   b. As the student gains familiarity with these two triads the instructor should gradually introduce the singing of triads beginning on other factors than the root.

   Instructor plays:

   Instructor announces that this is the fifth of the triad and asks the students to sing a major triad. The students sing:

   ```
        5   3   1   3   5
   ```

   c. When the student has gained a firm grasp of major and minor triads as outlined above, the instructor should involve him with more intricate procedures.

   Instructor plays:

   He then asks the students to consider this tone (1) as the root of a major triad, (2) as the third of a major triad, (3) as the fifth of a major triad. Students then sing:

   ```
   1  3  5  3  1   3  1  3  5  3   5  3  1  3  5
   ```

   This of course can be continued in the same vein using minor triads. Diminished and augmented triads should be introduced at the same time they are taken up in the Harmony Units.

d. The above procedures should be carried on to the limit of the students' capacities. Here is an illustration.

Instructor plays:

He then announces that this is the tonic degree of a scale and the students are asked to sing the I, IV, V, and I triad in this key. The student then sings:

1 3 5 3 1   1 3 5 3 1   1 3 5 3 1   1 3 5 3 1

The above drills are recommended to orient the student to the triads and various triad patterns. These should be initiated at the very beginning of the course in ear training. After a few days of such drills the instructor can safely begin the main body of Harmony Units as set forth in this text. The first few exercises are quite simple and should provide no difficulty even for the average or below average student.

Even though most of the exercises in the Harmony Units are self-explanatory, it should never be assumed that the student will immediately discover the most efficient and practical method of taking harmonic dictation. Much can be done by the instructor in class to assist the student in effecting an orderly and well organized procedure of dictation. Below are a few suggestions which will be of material aid to the student who has difficulty.

1. **Exercises of the type found in Harmony Unit No. 1, Section A.** In introducing this type of exercise it is wise to conduct a class drill having the student sing the tonic chord *between* each separate chord. Harmony Unit No. 1, Section A, Exercise No. 1 is used as an illustration. The instructor plays the four part harmony and the students sing the tonic note between each chord:

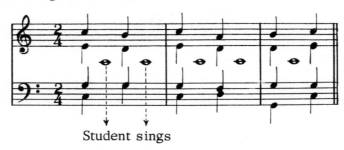

Student sings

Of course in this particular exercise the student is requested to identify only the tonic (I) triad. However, this type of exercise is found frequently in subsequent units where the student is asked to identify more and more of the triad vocabulary. As the exercises of this type become more complex a drill especially helpful is that of asking the student to sing the triad root immediately after each dictated chord. In this manner the student soon learns to sing (and to hear) the fundamental or root of each chord. Harmony Unit No. 6, Section A, Exercise 1 is used to illustrate:

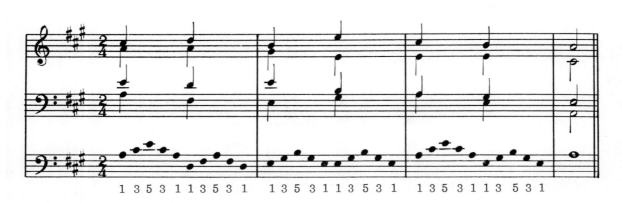

1 3 5 3 1 1 3 5 3 1   1 3 5 3 1 1 3 5 3 1   1 3 5 3 1 1 3 5 3 1

Students can soon learn to sing only:

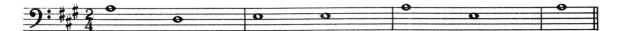

When the students increase their facility to the point that they can sing the root of each triad as it is played, they should then be able to identify the chord by its Roman Numeral analysis. As each new unit is taken up the instructor should illustrate in class the various separate steps necessary in achieving a smooth and orderly solution to the exercise.

2. **Exercises of the type found in Harmony Unit No. 1, Section C.** Experience has proven that students learn to identify chord factors in any given voice at any given time if they will learn to isolate the factor and sing the tone in its relationship to the entire harmonic structure at that point. The following class drill will increase the facility of establishing chord factors.

Instructor plays a triad in four part harmony:

Students first isolate and sing the soprano tone:

Students then sing the tone in relationship to the harmony.

Instructor then plays this same tone as another factor in another triad.

Students follow the procedure of isolating the soprano tone:

Students then sing the one in its new harmonic relationships:

Instructor continues the drill by playing the same soprano tone as yet a different factor:

Students follow the same procedure of isolating the soprano tone:

Students then sing the tone in its changed harmonic relationship:

This same procedure can be used in solving the chord factors in the bass (or any voice for that matter).

Instructor plays:

Student isolates the bass tone:

Students then sing the tone in relationship to the harmony:

3 1 3 5 3

If the student experiences difficulty in hearing either soprano or bass chord factors, the instructor should slow down dictation to the point that the above procedures can be manipulated meaningfully and without stress. However, the instructor should exert every encouragement for the student to increase his speed of operation.

3. **Exercises of the type found in Harmony Unit No. 5, Section D.** In this type of exercise the students are asked to write both the soprano and bass melody and make a complete analysis. Few are the students who can immediately accomplish this task in one hearing. Even with two hearings it is indeed difficult. Most students who encounter exercises of this type for the first time will need to break up the total operation into three distinct steps, as follows:

Step No. 1. Instructor plays:

Students determine the basic chord analysis on this first hearing:

1 3 5 3 1   1 3 5 3 1   1 3 5 3 1   1 3 5 3 1

Students then write:

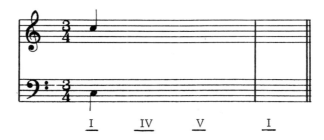

I   IV   V   I

Step 2. Instructor repeats:

Students determine the factor of each chord in the bass and write the bass melody:

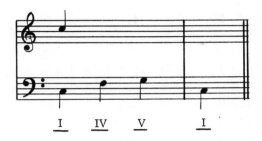

Step 3—Instructor plays for the third time:

Students determine the factor of each chord in the soprano and add the soprano notes to the staff:

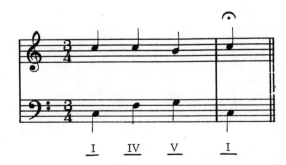

It must be remembered that drills of the various types listed above can be both a help and a hindrance. They can be a help if the students soon learn to increase the speed of the various steps and operations necessary to achieve the correct solutions. Ideally the students should gradually transcend the need for these pedagogical "crutches." The drills can actually result in impeding the quick and accurate solutions if the students are unable to divorce themselves from the involved procedure after a time. Students may come to rely completely on the burdensome and slow steps originally designed to organize and order their musical thinking, and they wind up in a hopeless entanglement of involved procedure.

The basic precepts discussed in the *Introduction* to Melody Units apply also to dictation procedures in Harmony Units. The instructor is at all times encouraged to use his imagination in helping the students to solve the ear training problems in all of the units. Each student is an individual, and no two students will approach the ear training work covered in this book in exactly the same manner. This challenges the instructor to assist each individual in solving his own individual problem. The successful instructor of ear training is the one who conceives his task as that of a consulting clinician who solves each individual student problem on an individual basis. It would be impossible here to explain and illustrate *all* of the clinical helps and guides which students may need from time to time in order to solve their problems in an efficient and systematized manner. Some of the class-tested procedures which have produced good results have been illustrated in this introduction. It is up to the good instructor to carry on from here.

HARMONY UNIT NO. 1

Workbook Page 92

A. RECOGNITION OF THE MAJOR TONIC TRIAD

To the Student: Each exercise is a series of triads (indicated by the numbers below).

Directions: Circle the numbers indicating the tonic (I) triads.

To the Teacher:
1. Before dictating the exercise play the tonic triad and have the students sing it (1 - 3 - 5 - 3 - 1, do - mi - so - mi - do, or using any other system you prefer).
2. Play the exercise at a speed of approximately one chord per 2 seconds.
3. For slower students have them sing the tonic triad after each chord is played. This procedure should be unnecessary as the students gain experience.

103

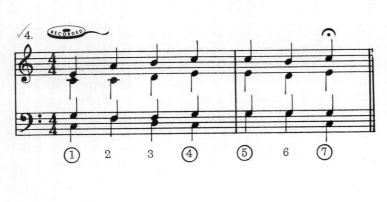

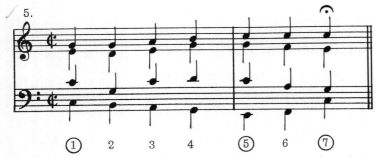

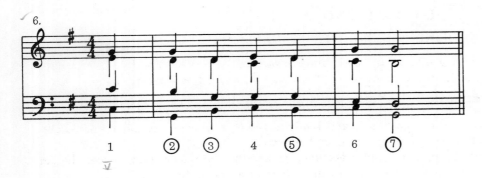

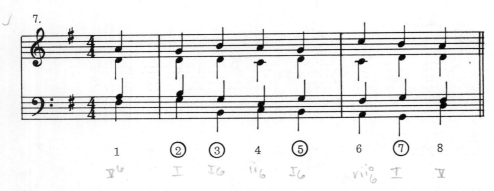

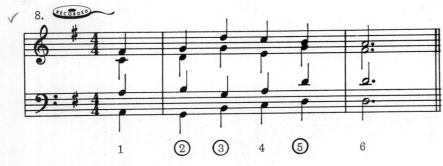

104

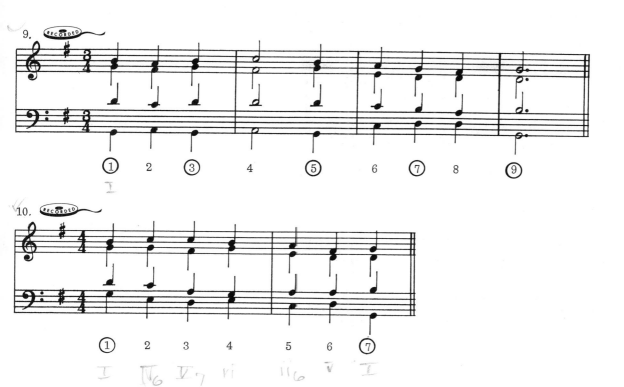

HARMONY UNIT NO. 1

Workbook Page 92

B. RECOGNITION OF THE MAJOR TRIAD

To the Student: The teacher will play a number of triads, some major and some not. The first 30 exercises are in simple three-note root position. The remaining 15 are in traditional four-part harmony.

Directions: Circle the number of the triads which are major in sound. Do not mark the others.

To the Teacher: If the students name the major triads accurately in the first 10 exercises move immediately to exercise 31 where the triads are spaced in four-part harmony.
If the first 30 exercises are not sufficient to obtain accuracy in hearing the major triad, repeat the set backwards from 30 through 1 and ask the students to give their answers orally.

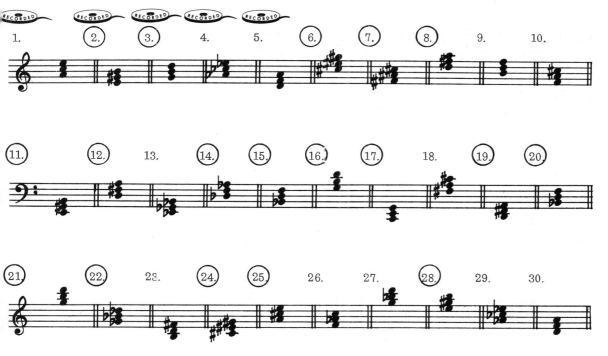

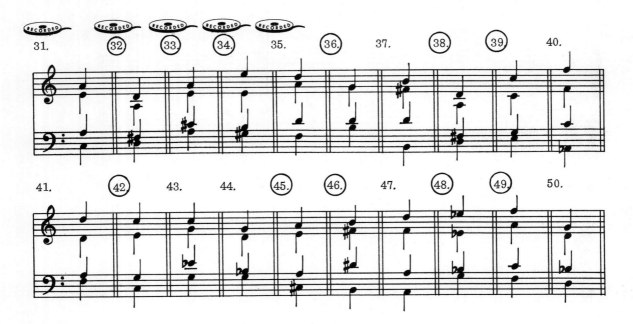

HARMONY UNIT NO. 1

Workbook Page 92

C. RECOGNITION OF TRIAD FACTOR IN THE SOPRANO

To the Student: The teacher will play a triad in simple three-note position. Sing this triad exactly as he plays it—1 - 3 - 5 - 3 - 1. He will then play the same triad in four part harmony after which he will play only the soprano note. Sing the soprano note after he plays it. Then:

Directions: Circle the chord factor you hear in the soprano voice.

To the Teacher: First play the triad in simple position as shown. Have the students sing this triad immediately using the factor numbers 1 - 3 - 5 - 3 - 1.

Then, play the four part version of the same triad. Immediately play the soprano note alone. Have the students sing this soprano note and determine which of the factors it is.

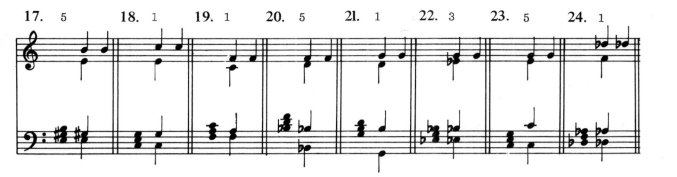

17. 5   18. 1   19. 1   20. 5   21. 1   22. 3   23. 5   24. 1

Workbook Page 93

HARMONY UNIT NO. 1
D. PLACING SOPRANO FACTORS ON THE STAFF

To the Student: Below you see a series of major triads in simple position, and immediately following each triad is a bass note.

Directions:
1. The teacher will play the triad in simple position. Sing the triad.
2. The teacher will then play this same triad in a four-part arrangement. Sing the soprano note.
3. Determine the factor of the soprano note.
4. **In these exercises the bass note is always the root of the triad.** Determine the soprano *note* and write it on the staff immediately above the bass note.

To the Teacher: These exercises are for the student to relate the soprano factor NUMBER to the correct soprano PITCH.

The student will have had practice determining soprano factor numbers in Harmony Unit No. 1, Section C. After he has determined the correct factor number he must then relate it to a specific triad (as listed in each exercise).
1. Play the simple position of the triad. Have the student sing this.
2. Play the triad in four-part harmony. Have the student sing the soprano note.
3. Have the students use factor numbers (1 - 3 - 5), and compare the soprano factor with the bass (which in this case is always 1).
4. When these numbers are transferred to actual pitches the student is then ready to write the soprano note.

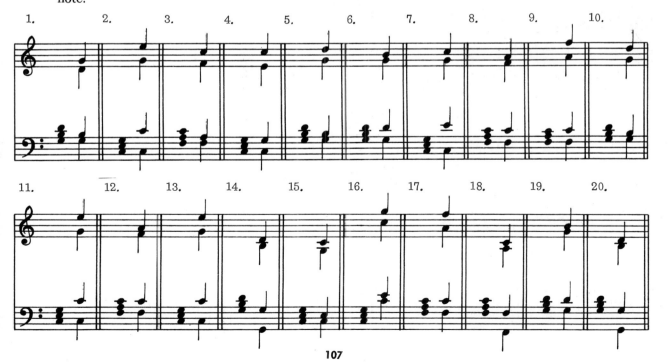

107

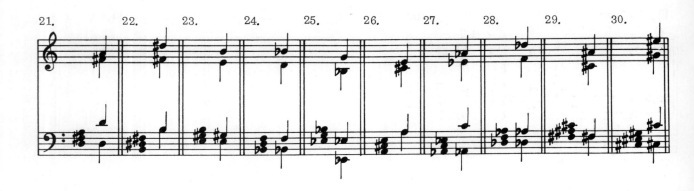

HARMONY UNIT NO. 2

A. RECOGNITION OF THE MINOR TONIC TRIAD

To the Student: Each exercise is a series of triads (indicated by the numbers below). All are in a minor key.
  Directions: Circle the numbers indicating the tonic (I) triads.

To the Teacher:
1. Before dictating the exercise play the minor tonic triad and have the students sing it (1 - 3 - 5 - 3 - 1, la - do - mi - do - la, or using any other system you prefer).
2. Play the exercise at a speed of approximately one chord per 2 seconds.
3. For slower students have them sing the tonic triad after each chord is played (for comparison). This procedure should be unnecessary as the students gain experience.

4.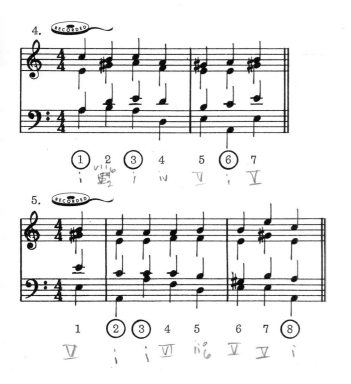

5.

6. Bach--Es Stehn Vor Gottes Throne

7. Bach--Schaut, Ihr Sunder

8. Bach--Sei Gegrusset, Jesu Gütig

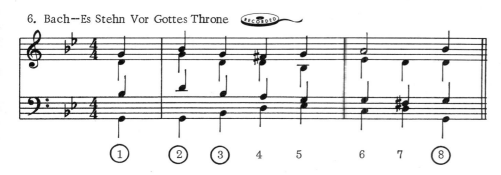
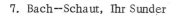
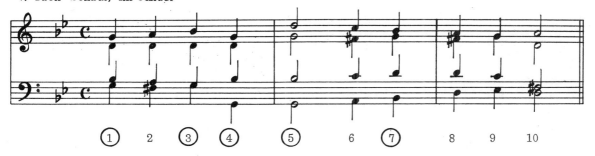
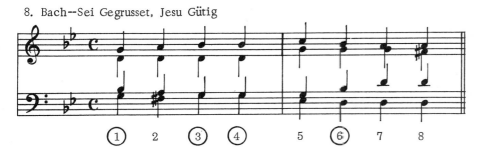

HARMONY UNIT NO. 2
B. RECOGNITION OF THE MINOR TRIAD

To the Student: Each exercise consists of a single triad. The first 10 exercises are triads in simple three-note position. The remaining 30 are in four-part harmony, all in root position (root is the bass note).

Directions: Circle the numbers of the triads which are minor in sound. Do not mark the others.

To the Teacher: The students will find the first 10 exercises easier because they are in simple three-note position. Students who have difficulty recognizing the minor triad should *sing* each exercise after it is played. In the exercises from No. 11 through No. 40 the students should sing the triads in simple three-note position.

HARMONY UNIT NO. 2
C. RECOGNITION OF THE TRIAD FACTOR IN THE SOPRANO

To the Student: The teacher will play a triad in simple three-note position. *Sing* this triad exactly as he plays it—1 - 3 - 5 - 3 - 1. He will then play the same triad in four part harmony. Immediately *sing* the soprano note and determine which factor it is (either 1 or 3 or 5).

Directions: Circle the chord factor you hear in the soprano voice.

To the Teacher: First play the triad in simple position as shown. Have the students sing this triad immediately using the factor numbers 1 - 3 - 5 - 3 - 1.
Then, play the four part version of the same triad. Immediately, have the students single out the soprano note and *sing* it. Have the students determine which factor the soprano note is by having them compare it with the simple triad they sang. If some students have difficulty with this procedure have them sing *again* the simple triad and then the soprano note until the comparison is clear in their mind.

HARMONY UNIT NO. 2

D. RECOGNITION OF OPEN AND CLOSE POSITION

To the Student: Each exercise is a single triad in four part harmony. Listen carefully to determine whether the chord is in open or close position.

OPEN POSITION—*more* than an octave spacing between the tenor and the soprano.

CLOSE POSITION—*less* than an octave spacing between the tenor and soprano.

Directions:
1. Mark "O" if the chord is in open position.
2. Mark "C" if the chord is in close position.

To the Teacher:
1. Make sure all students understand the terms.
2. Play the chords. With the first two or three, emphasize the tenor and soprano voice to give the students a special opportunity to form a judgment. Then, with each next chord gradually balance the voices.

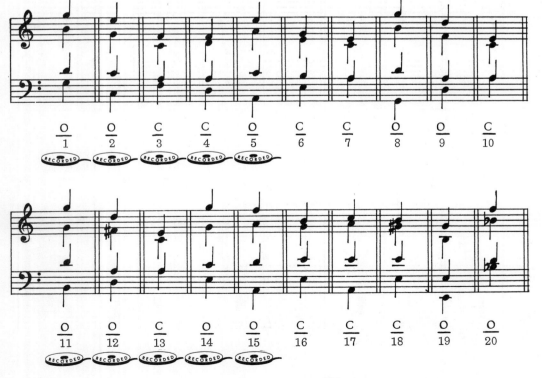

112

HARMONY UNIT NO. 3
A. RECOGNITION OF THE I AND V TRIAD

To the Student: The following series of chord progressions (indicated by numbers below) contain *only* the I and V triads.

Directions:

1. Place a "I" above those numbers which stand for tonic triads.
2. Place a "V" above those numbers which stand for dominant triads.

To the Teacher:

1. Play the tonic triad and have the students sing it.
2. Play the dominant triad and have the students sing it.
3. Play the exercise, chord by chord, and after each chord have the students sing the triad (in root position).
4. When the students have sufficiently grasped this procedure they may then write their answers on paper. This procedure should be abandoned after a few exercises.

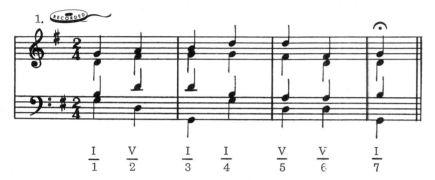

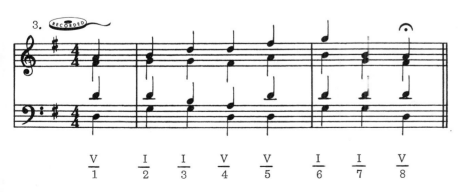

HARMONY UNIT NO. 3
B. RECOGNITION OF THE I AND V TRIAD

To the Student: The following series of chord progressions (indicated by numbers below) contain the I and V triads in addition to other triads which are neither I nor V.

Directions:
1. Place a "I" above those numbers which stand for tonic triads.
2. Place a "V" above those numbers which stand for dominant triads.
3. Leave blank any numbers which are neither I nor V.

To the Teacher: Use the same procedure for dictating as was used in the previous section (Harmony Unit No. 3, Section A). The section below (here) is the same as Section A except that other triads are added —in addition to the I and V triads.

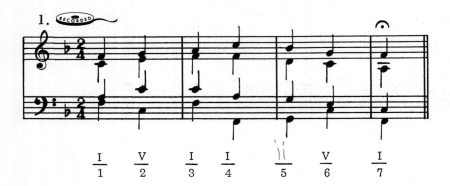

HARMONY UNIT NO. 3
C. RECOGNIZING THE MAJOR AND MINOR TRIAD

To the Student: Each exercise consists of one triad played in four-part harmony. It will be either a major triad or a minor triad.

Directions: Write large "M" if the triad is major. Write small "m" if the triad is minor.

To the Teacher: After playing each triad have the students sing it in simple three-note position.

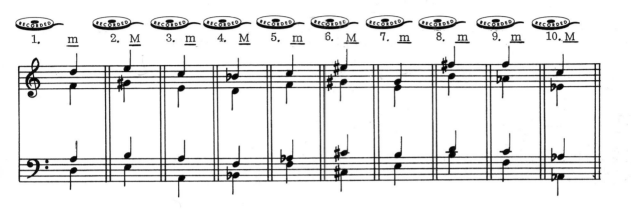

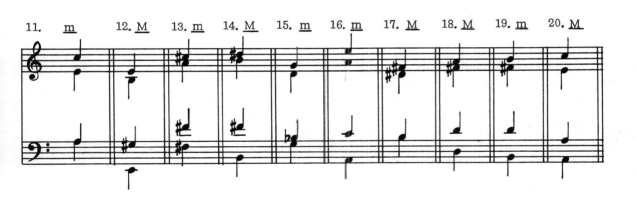

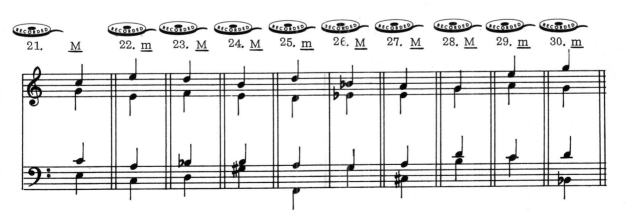

HARMONY UNIT NO. 3

D. TRIAD FACTORS IN THE BASS VOICE

To the Student: Each exercise consists of a single triad played in four-part harmony. Listen carefully for the bass note.

Directions:
1. The teacher plays a triad in four-part harmony. Sing the triad in its simple three-note position.
2. The teacher plays the triad again, emphasizing the bass note slightly. Sing the bass note.
3. Compare the bass note you just sang with the three factors (1 - 3 - 5) you sang earlier.
4. WRITE THE FACTOR YOU HEAR IN THE BASS VOICE.

To the Teacher: Be sure the student can sing the triad in simple three-note position before trying to determine the factor in the bass.

After he sings the triad in simple three-note position play the triad again in four-part harmony. Make sure the student can sing the bass note. He is then ready to place his answer on the page.

116

HARMONY UNIT NO. 4

A. RECOGNITION OF THE I, V, AND VII TRIAD

To the Student: Each exercise consists of four possible chord progressions, Column 1, Column 2, Column 3, and Column 4. The instructor plays one of the four.

Directions: Circle the correct chord progression (in Column 1, Column 2, Column 3, or Column 4).

To the Teacher:
1. Play the tonic note and have the students sing the I, V, and VII triads before dictating the exercises.
2. Play each exercise at an approximate speed of one chord per 2 seconds.

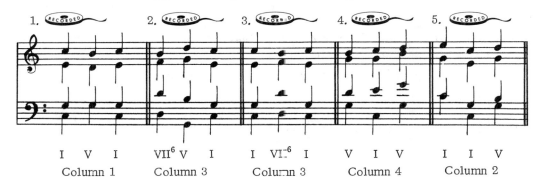

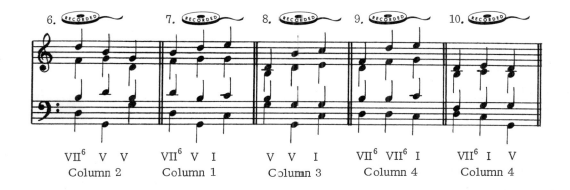

HARMONY UNIT NO. 4

B. RECOGNITION OF THE I, V, AND VII⁶ TRIADS

To the Student: Each exercise contains only the I, V, and VII⁶ triads. The numbers (below) indicate the chords you will hear.

Directions:
1. Place a (I) above those numbers that are tonic triads.
2. Place a (V) above those numbers that are dominant triads.
3. Place a (VII⁶) above those numbers that are the leading tone triad in first inversion.

To the Teacher:
1. Play the tonic note and have the students sing the I, V, and VII⁶ triads.
2. Play the exercises at an approximate speed of one chord per 2 seconds.

1.

I   VII⁶   I   I   V   V   I

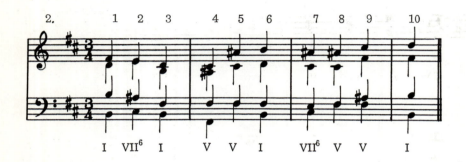

2.

I   VII⁶   I   V   V   I   VII⁶   V   V   I

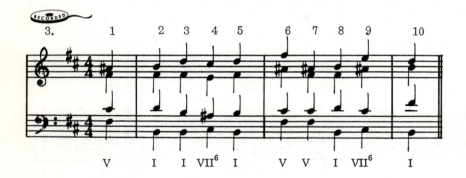

3.

V   I   I   VII⁶   I   V   V   I   VII⁶   I

Workbook Page 99

HARMONY UNIT NO. 4

C. IMPLIED HARMONY IN TWO VOICE WRITING. I, IV, V.

To the Student: Each exercise consists of four two-part sonorities which imply triads. Only the I, IV, and V triads will be implied in these exercises. Two harmonic voices can never state all three tones of a triad, but common usage has conditioned listeners to assume the function of a triad when only two voices are given. Here are examples of two voices that imply triads:

CM: I   I   I   I   I⁶   IV   IV   IV   IV   IV⁶   V   V   V   V   V

Directions:
1. Write the upper voice on the staff in notation.
2. Write the lower voice on the staff in notation.
3. Write the harmonic analysis of the implied triads in the blanks below each staff.

To the Teacher:

1. Play the exercise emphasizing the upper voice slightly.
2. Play the exercise emphasizing the lower voice slightly.
3. Play each harmonic interval separately.
4. Have the students immediately sing the complete triad (in simple three note position, root as lowest note) which is implied.
5. When students can do this accurately they are ready to complete the harmonic analysis.

The first notes and analysis in each exercise are given in Student Workbook.

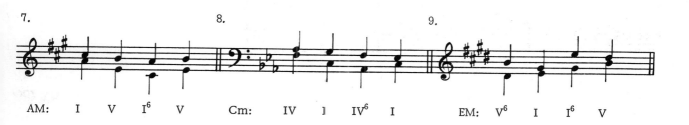

HARMONY UNIT NO. 4

D. RECOGNITION OF THE MAJOR, MINOR, AND DIMINISHED TRIAD

To the Student: Each exercise consists of three triads—a major triad, a minor triad, and a diminished triad (all in four part harmony). The instructor plays only one of these three possibilities.

Directions: Circle the letter indicating the chord played by the instructor.

To the Teacher:
1. Have the students sing all three possibilities in simple (three note, root position) position.
2. Play the chord (correct answer) and have the students immediately sing it.
3. Have students then write their answer on paper.

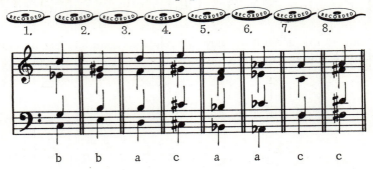

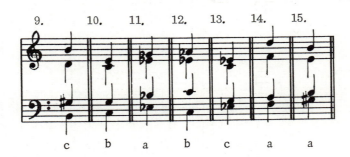

HARMONY UNIT NO. 4

Workbook Page 100

E. SOPRANO FACTORS AND CHORD ANALYSIS

To the Student: The teacher will play the phrases below in four-part harmony. Numbers 1 and 2 have only the soprano missing, Number 3 is missing two voices, and Number 4 supplies only a few notes here and there.

Directions:

Numbers 1 & 2: Determine the factor of the chord which is in the soprano and write the note on the staff.

Make a Roman Numeral analysis of each chord.

Number 3: Determine the bass factor and write the analysis of the chord. The instructor will emphasize the bass tone.

Determine the factor of the chord in the soprano, and then from the analysis of the chord, determine the soprano note. Write it on the staff.

Number 4: See if you can determine the complete Soprano melody, the Bass melody, and the analysis from the information given.

To the Teacher:

Numbers 1 & 2: Play each chord slowly enough for the student to hear each chord separately. If students have difficulty with the procedure listed above, have them sing each chord in simple three-note position and compare the soprano note with the three factors they sing.

Number 3: The procedure here is essentially the same as for No. 1 & 2, but it is a greater challenge for the better student.

Number 4: The superior students should have no difficulty with this exercise. Emphasize the soprano notes on two playings, and the bass notes on two other playings.

"×" indicates notes missing in student workbook.

HARMONY UNIT NO. 5

A. RECOGNITION OF THE I, V, VII⁶, AND IV TRIAD

To the Student: A series of correct but scrambled analyses is given. Look at the series and try to determine the proper order.

Directions: Place the chords in their proper order in the blanks provided.

To the Teacher: These may be dictated at a faster speed than most other harmonic dictation drills—especially those requiring the student to write notes on the staff.

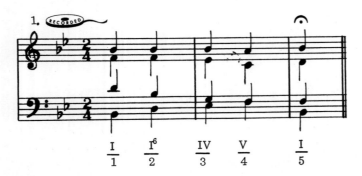

$$\frac{\text{I}}{1} \quad \frac{\text{I}^6}{2} \quad \frac{\text{IV}}{3} \quad \frac{\text{V}}{4} \quad \frac{\text{I}}{5}$$

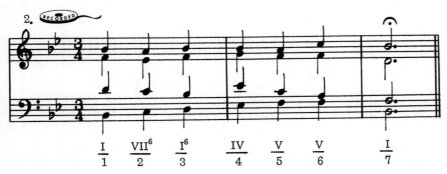

$$\frac{\text{I}}{1} \quad \frac{\text{VII}^6}{2} \quad \frac{\text{I}^6}{3} \quad \frac{\text{IV}}{4} \quad \frac{\text{V}}{5} \quad \frac{\text{V}}{6} \quad \frac{\text{I}}{7}$$

$$\frac{\text{V}}{1} \quad \frac{\text{I}^6}{2} \quad \frac{\text{I}}{3} \quad \frac{\text{VII}^6}{4} \quad \frac{\text{I}^6}{5} \quad \frac{\text{IV}}{6} \quad \frac{\text{V}}{7} \quad \frac{\text{I}}{8}$$

$$\frac{\text{I}^6}{1} \quad \frac{\text{VII}^6}{2} \quad \frac{\text{V}}{3} \quad \frac{\text{I}^6}{4} \quad \frac{\text{IV}}{5} \quad \frac{\text{V}}{6} \quad \frac{\text{I}}{7} \quad \frac{\text{V}}{8}$$

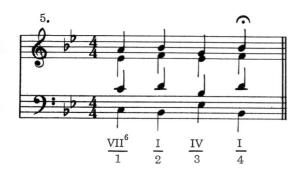

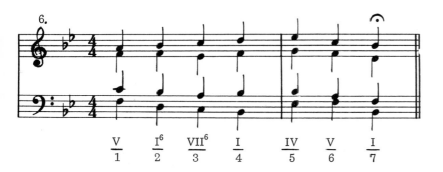

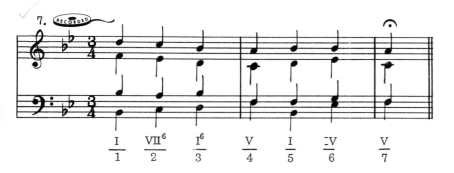

HARMONY UNIT NO. 5

Workbook Page 102

B. RECOGNIZING SOPRANO AND BASS FACTORS

To the Student: The teacher will play a short phrase of music which includes several different triads. Listen carefully to both the soprano and bass notes.

Directions:
1. The teacher emphasizes the soprano note of each chord. Sing the soprano note, relate it to the remainder of the triad, and write the soprano factor in the blank provided.
2. The teacher emphasizes the bass note of each chord. Sing the bass note, relate it to the remainder of the triad, and write the bass factor in the blank provided.

Optional:
3. If from the above information you can also calculate the ANALYSIS of the chords, write the analysis in the third row of blanks.

To the Teacher:
1. Play each set of chords (about one chord per two or three seconds) emphasizing the *soprano* the first and second time.
2. Play each set of chords (about one chord per two or three seconds) emphasizing the *bass* the third and fourth time.

If necessary (for students who have difficulty) have the students sing each chord in simple three-note position before going on to the next chord. Most students by now will have gained enough facility to by-pass this helpful crutch.

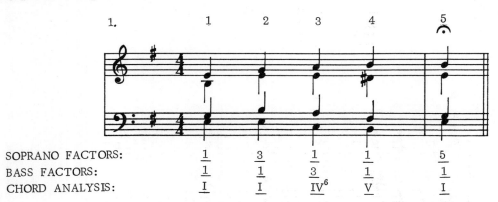

	1	2	3	4	5
SOPRANO FACTORS:	1	3	1	1	5
BASS FACTORS:	1	1	3	1	1
CHORD ANALYSIS:	I	I	IV⁶	V	I

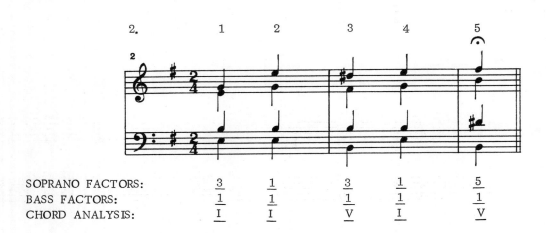

	1	2	3	4	5
SOPRANO FACTORS:	3	1	3	1	5
BASS FACTORS:	1	1	1	1	1
CHORD ANALYSIS:	I	I	V	I	V

	1	2	3	4
SOPRANO FACTORS:	1	3	3	3
BASS FACTORS:	3	1	3	1
CHORD ANALYSIS:	V⁶	I	VII⁶	I

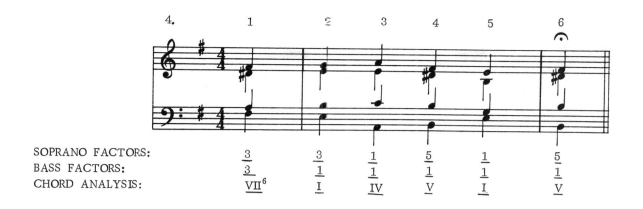

4.

SOPRANO FACTORS:	$\frac{3}{3}$	$\frac{3}{1}$	$\frac{1}{1}$	$\frac{5}{1}$	$\frac{1}{1}$	$\frac{5}{1}$
BASS FACTORS:						
CHORD ANALYSIS:	$\underline{VII}^6$	$\underline{I}$	$\underline{IV}$	$\underline{V}$	$\underline{I}$	$\underline{V}$

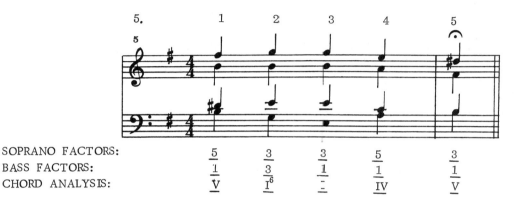

5.

SOPRANO FACTORS:	$\frac{5}{1}$	$\frac{3}{3}$	$\frac{3}{1}$	$\frac{5}{1}$	$\frac{3}{1}$
BASS FACTORS:					
CHORD ANALYSIS:	$\underline{V}$	$\underline{I}^6$	$\underline{-}$	$\underline{IV}$	$\underline{V}$

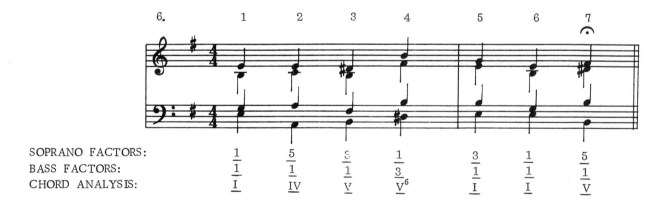

6.

SOPRANO FACTORS:	$\frac{1}{1}$	$\frac{5}{1}$	$\frac{3}{1}$	$\frac{1}{3}$	$\frac{3}{1}$	$\frac{1}{1}$	$\frac{5}{1}$
BASS FACTORS:							
CHORD ANALYSIS:	$\underline{I}$	$\underline{IV}$	$\underline{V}$	$\underline{V}^6$	$\underline{I}$	$\underline{I}$	$\underline{V}$

7. Bach—Nun Freut Euch, Lieben Christen Cmein

SOPRANO FACTORS:	$\frac{1}{1}$	$\frac{1}{3}$	$\frac{1}{1}$	$\frac{1}{3}$	$\frac{5}{3}$	$\frac{3}{1}$	$\frac{5}{1}$	$\frac{1}{1}$
BASS FACTORS:								
CHORD ANALYSIS:	$\underline{I}$	$\underline{I}^6$	$\underline{V}$	$\underline{I}^6$	$\underline{VII}^6$	$\underline{I}$	$\underline{V}$	$\underline{I}$

8. Bach—Der Tag Der 1st So Freudenreich

	1	2	3	4	5	6	7	8
SOPRANO FACTORS:	1	3	5	1	3	1	5	1
BASS FACTORS:	1	1	1	1	1	1	1	1
CHORD ANALYSIS:	I	VI	IV	II	I	IV	V	I

Workbook Page 104

HARMONY UNIT NO. 5

C. RECOGNITION OF THE MAJOR, MINOR AND DIMINISHED TRIADS

To the Student: Each triad you hear in the following series is either a major, minor, or diminished triad.

Directions:

1. Write *M* for major triad, *m* for minor triad, and *d* for diminished triad in the proper blanks.

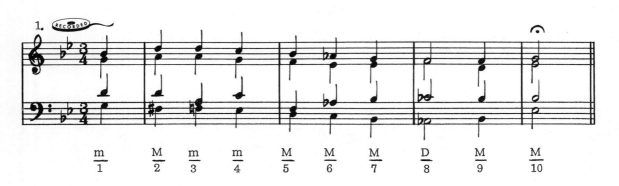

m	M	m	m	M	M	M	D	M	M
1	2	3	4	5	6	7	8	9	10

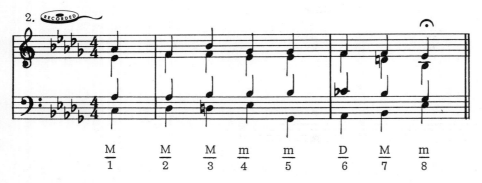

M	M	M	m	m	D	M	m
1	2	3	4	5	6	7	8

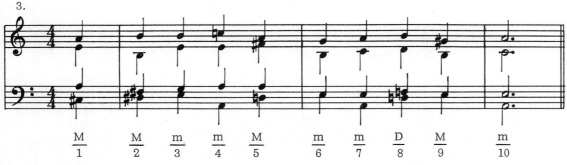

M	M	m	m	M	m	m	D	M	m
1	2	3	4	5	6	7	8	9	10

HARMONY UNIT NO. 5
D. DICTATION OF I, V, VII, AND IV TRIADS

To the Student: The teacher will play a phrase of music in four-part harmony.

Directions:
1. The teacher will emphasize the soprano melody the first time or two. WRITE THE MELODY ON THE STAFF.
2. The teacher will emphasize the bass notes next. WRITE THE BASS NOTES ON THE STAFF.
3. The teacher will play each chord slowly with all voices balanced. Sing each chord in simple three-note position. Determine whether the chord is I, V, VII, or IV. WRITE THE ANALYSIS UNDER THE BASS NOTES.
4. DETERMINE THE POSITION (whether root, third, or fifth is the bass note) and indicate that in the analysis. Use "6" for first inversion and "6/4" for second inversion.

To the Teacher:
1. Play the exercise emphasizing the soprano once or twice.
2. Play the exercise emphasizing the bass once or twice.
3. Play each chord with all voices balanced—for analysis.
4. For special drill with students having difficulty, have the student sing the *root* of each chord as you play it. Then, have him sing the roots of all the chords in the exercise in rapid succession.
5. Student Workbook has bass and soprano given in first chord.

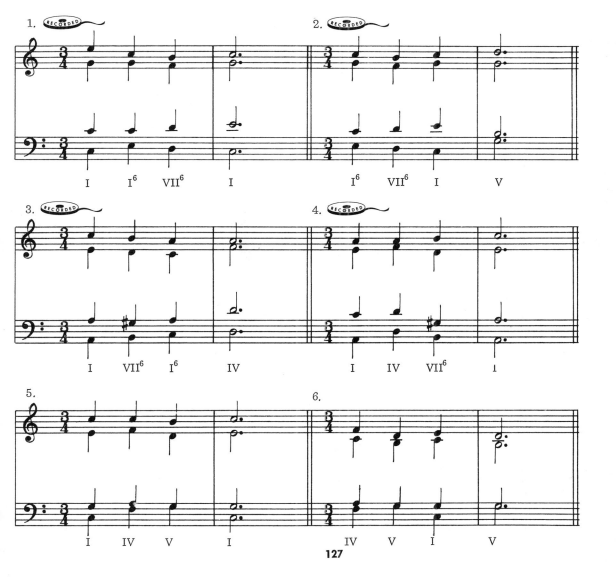

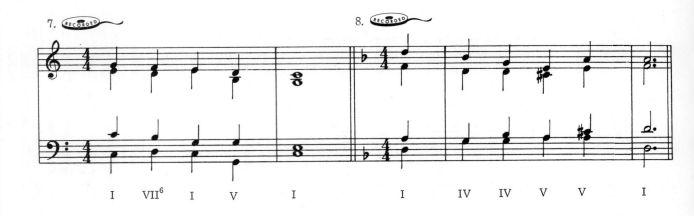

Workbook Page 107

HARMONY UNIT NO. 6

A. RECOGNITION OF THE I, V, VII⁶ AND IV TRIADS

To the Student: Each exercise is a complete phrase in four part writing. Some of the notes are missing. The instructor will play the entire phrase—listen for the missing notes.

Directions:
1. Add the complete melody in the soprano.
2. Add the complete melody in the bass.
3. Make a complete harmonic analysis of the entire exercise.

Optional:
4. In addition to the above add also the tenor and alto voices.

To the Teacher:

1. Play once or twice emphasizing the soprano voice.
2. Play once or twice emphasizing the bass voice.
3. Play once slightly slower for student analysis of each chord.

*"×" indicates note which is missing in Student Manual. When the sign is above a chord it indicates the entire chord is missing.

129

5.

| I | V | IV | VII⁶ | I | V⁶ | V | I |

6.

| I | VII⁶ | I⁶ | I | IV⁶ | V⁶ | I |

Workbook Page 109

HARMONY UNIT NO. 6

B. RECOGNITION OF SOPRANO AND BASS FACTORS

To the Student: The teacher will play a short phrase of music in four-part harmony.

Directions:
1. The teacher will emphasize the soprano notes. Sing the chord in its simple three-note position, and compare the soprano note with the others you sing. Write the soprano factor in the space provided.
2. The teacher will emphasize the bass notes. Sing the chord in its simple three-note position, and compare the bass note with the others you sing. Write the bass factor in the space provided.

Optional:
3. See if you can also write the correct analysis of each chord.

To the Teacher: Many students by now will be able to write the soprano and bass factors without having to sing the triad in simple three-note position. Others may still require the customary crutches. Hopefully all students will increase their speed of perception. For those who still lag behind previous exercises emphasizing soprano and bass factors should be repeated.

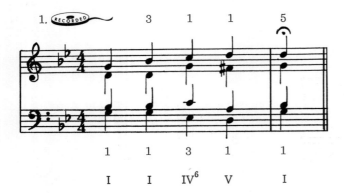

1.

	3	1	1	5

1	1	3	1	1

| I | I | IV⁶ | V | I |

130

2. RECORDED

V⁶   I   VII⁶   I

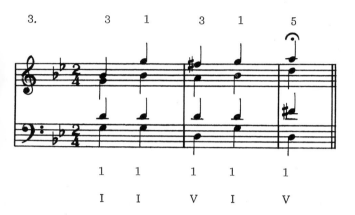

3.

I   I   V   I   V

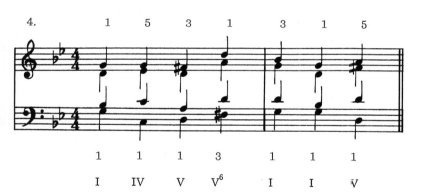

4.

I   IV   V   V⁶   I   I   V̄

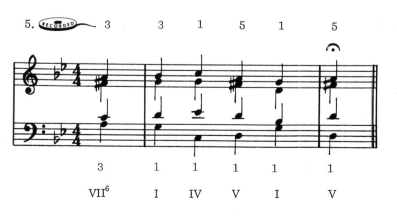

5. RECORDED

VII⁶   I   IV   V   I   V

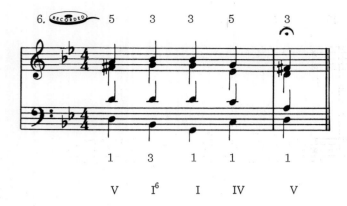

HARMONY UNIT NO. 6

C. RECOGNIZING AND WRITING MAJOR, MINOR, AND DIMINISHED TRIADS

To the Student: Each exercise is a single triad—either major, minor, or diminished.

Directions:
Numbers 1-10—A triad in simple three-note position is played. The given note is the ROOT of the triad. Write the remainder of the triad on the staff.

Numbers 11-20—A triad in simple three-note position is played. The given note is the THIRD of the triad. Write the remainder of the triad on the staff.

Numbers 21-30—A triad in four-part harmony is played. The given note is the ROOT of this triad. Although the triad is played in four-part harmony write it on the staff in simple three-note position.

Numbers 31-40—A triad in four-part harmony is played. The given note is the THIRD of this triad. Although the triad is played in four-part harmony write it on the staff in simple three-note position.

To the Teacher: Some students may still need to sing the triad after it is played although most will be able to bypass this aid.

With exercises 21 through 40 it may be wise to have the students sing the triad in simple three-note position before writing it on the staff.

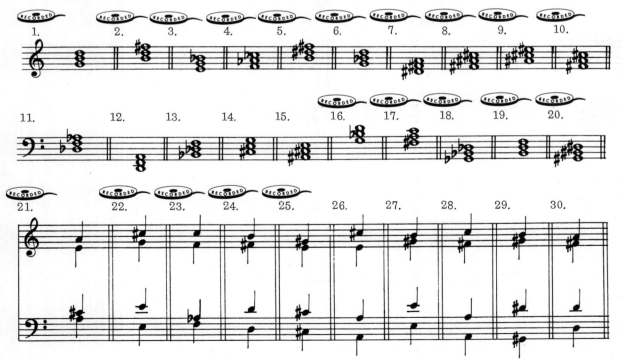

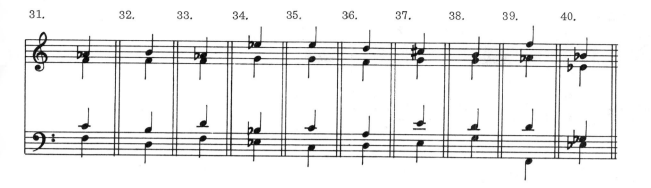

31. 32. 33. 34. 35. 36. 37. 38. 39. 40.

Workbook Page 111

HARMONY UNIT NO. 6
D. DICTATION OF THE I, V, VII⁶, AND IV TRIADS

To the Student: In each of the four part harmony exercises below there are missing notes.

Directions:
1. Add the missing parts.
2. Make a complete harmonic analysis.

To the Teacher: Play each exercise at an approximate speed of one chord per two seconds. Finally, play each chord slightly slower for harmonic analysis.

*"×" indicates note which is missing in Student Manual.

4.

I V IV⁶ V⁶ I I⁶₄ V I

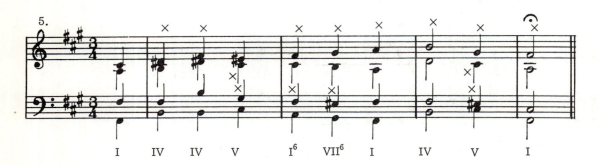

5.

I IV IV V I⁶ VII⁶ I IV V I

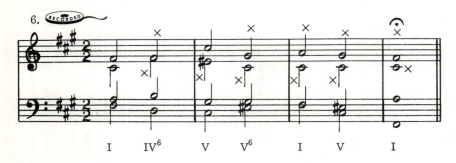

6.

I IV⁶ V V⁶ I V I

HARMONY UNIT NO. 7

A. RECOGNITION OF THE I, V, VII⁶, IV, AND II TRIADS

To the Student: Each exercise consists of four possible chord progressions, Column 1, Column 2, Column 3, and Column 4. The instructor plays one of the four.

Directions: Circle the correct chord progression (in Column 1, Column 2, Column 3, or Column 4).

To the Teacher:
1. Play the tonic note and have the students sing the I, V, VII, IV, and II triads.
2. Then, play the exercises.

1.

I I⁶ V I
Column 3

2.

I IV I V
Column 4

135

13.

14.

I⁶   IV   II   V   VII⁶   I⁶   II   V
Column 2   Column 4

15.

16.

V⁶   IV⁶   I ⁶₄   V   IV⁶   II⁶   VII⁶   I
Column 1   Column 2

HARMONY UNIT NO. 7

Workbook Page 113

B. DICTATION OF BASS AND SOPRANO MELODY LINE

To the Student: In each of the four-part exercises below the bass and soprano voice is missing.

Directions:
1. The teacher will emphasize the soprano melody. Write the soprano melody on the staff.
2. The teacher will emphasize the bass melody. Write the bass melody on the staff.
3. Make an analysis of each chord in the blanks provided.

To the Teacher:
1. Play the soprano melody slowly and have the students sing it back to you immediately. After the students have the melody well in mind they should then write it.
2. Use the same procedure for the bass melody.
3. Allow the students time to complete the analysis before moving on to the next exercise.

Bass and soprano voices are missing in Student Workbook.

1. RECORDED

I   V⁶   I   VII⁶   I⁶   II⁶   V

2.

I   IV   VII⁶   I⁶   I   II   I⁶   V   I

HARMONY UNIT NO. 7

C. RECOGNITION OF THE I, V, VII⁶, IV, AND II TRIAD

To the Student: The instructor will play a four part harmonic phrase. The first bass and soprano note is given.

Directions:

1. Write the soprano notes on the staff.
2. Write the bass notes on the staff.
3. Make a complete harmonic analysis of all chords.

Optional:

4. In addition to the above, also add the alto and tenor voice.

To the Teacher:

1. Play once or twice emphasizing the soprano.
2. Play once or twice emphasizing the bass.
3. Play once slightly slower for students to make an analysis.

Bass and soprano of first chord is given in Student Workbook.

1.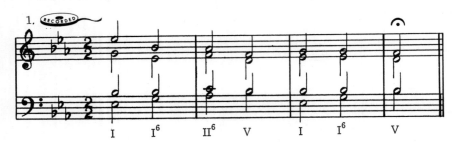

    I   I⁶   II⁶   V   I   I⁶   V

2.

    I⁶   V   II⁶   I⁶   IV   I⁵   VII⁶   I   II⁶   V   I

3.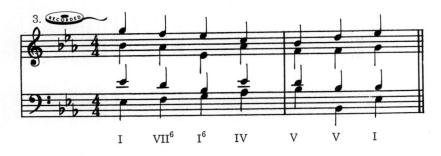

    I   VII⁶   I⁶   IV   V   V   I

4.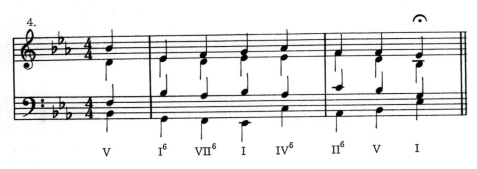

    V   I⁶   VII⁶   I   IV⁶   II⁶   V   I

5.

    I⁶   V   VII⁶   I⁶   I   IV   IV   I

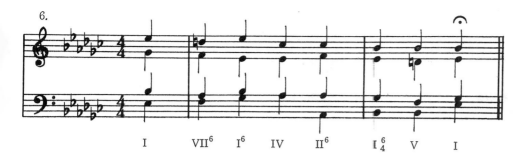

I   VII⁶   I⁶   IV   II⁶   I$_4^6$ V   I

HARMONY UNIT NO. 7

D. RECOGNITION OF ERRORS IN FOUR-PART WRITING

To the Student: In the following exercises the printed notes you see are correct. However, the teacher will play a version which contains errors.

Numbers 1 through 18—Contains two chords only. *One* error in the second chord in each exercise.

Numbers 19 through 24—Each exercise contains from seven to ten chords. The number of errors in each exercise is stated above the exercise.

Directions: Place a circle around the notes below which have been incorrectly played.

To the Teacher: Play the exercises at a speed of one chord per second. Arpeggiate (roll) the chords if necessary at first. This procedure is easier for the students. However, gradually alter this type of dictation so that a simultaneous playing of all chord tones is soon brought about.

*These circles indicate the notes which differ from those in the Student Workbook.

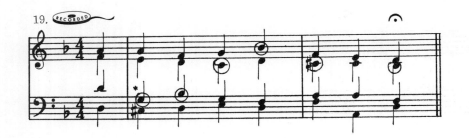

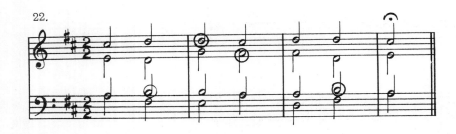

24.

HARMONY UNIT NO. 8

A. RECOGNITION OF THE PASSING TONE, NEIGHBORING TONE, AND ANTICIPATION

To the Student: The following four part harmonizations are correct except they lack the non-harmonic tones mentioned above. The instructor will play the phrase *with* non-harmonic tones.

Directions: Add the non-harmonic tones as played by the instructor.

To the Teacher: Play each exercise at a comfortable speed slightly faster than that used in dictating two or four part dictation.

HARMONY UNIT NO. 8

Workbook Page 120

B. FOUR PART DICTATION

To the Student: The instructor will play a phrase in four part harmony. Some of the chords are missing in the copy below.

Directions: Add all missing notes (four parts) as played by the instructor.

To the Teacher: The student should be encouraged to combine logic with ear training. As he tries to determine the four part arrangement he should think in terms of probabilities instead of possibilities. At first it may be necessary to "roll" the missing chords, but this practice should be eliminated as soon as possible.

*"×" indicates chord omitted in Student Workbook.

143

HARMONY UNIT NO. 8

C. RECOGNIZING AND WRITING MAJOR, MINOR, AND DIMINISHED TRIADS

To the Student: Each exercise is a single triad—either major, minor, or diminished.

Directions:

Numbers 1-10—A triad in simple position is played. The given note is the ROOT of the triad. Write the remainder of the triad on the staff.

Numbers 11-20—A triad in simple position is played. The given note is the FIFTH of the triad. Write the remainder of the triad on the staff.

Numbers 21-30—A triad in four-part harmony is played. The given note is the ROOT of this triad. Although the triad is played in four-part harmony write it on the staff in simple three-note position.

Numbers 31-40—A triad in four-part harmony is played. The given note is the FIFTH of this triad. Although the triad is played in four-part harmony write it on the staff in simple three-note position.

To the Teacher: Some students may still need to sing the triad after it is played although most will be able to bypass this aid. If students have difficulty with exercises 21 through 40 have them sing the triad in simple three-note position before writing it on the staff.

HARMONY UNIT NO. 8

D. RECOGNITION OF THE I, V, VII⁶, IV, AND II TRIAD

To the Student: The instructor will play a series of four part chords. Only the I, V, VII, IV, and II triad will be played (any may be in inversion, however).

Directions: Write the correct Roman Numeral to indicate the chord. Each blank indicates a chord. Disregard inversions in your analysis—you need not indicate inversions.

To the Teacher: Generally you will find a speed of one chord per two seconds to be adequate for most students, but it is wise to experiment with faster speeds to encourage more rapid response.

5.

I V IV VII⁶ I II V I

6.

I I I V⁶ V V⁶ I⁶ I IV⁶ V

Workbook Page 124

HARMONY UNIT NO. 9

A. RECOGNITION OF THE SUSPENSION, ESCAPE TONE, AND APPOGGIATURA

To the Student: The following four part harmonizations are correct except that they lack the non-harmonic tones mentioned above. The instructor will play the phrase *with* non-harmonic tones.

Directions: Add the non-harmonic tones as played by the instructor.

To the Teacher: Play each exercise at a comfortable speed slightly faster than that used in dictating two or four part dictation.

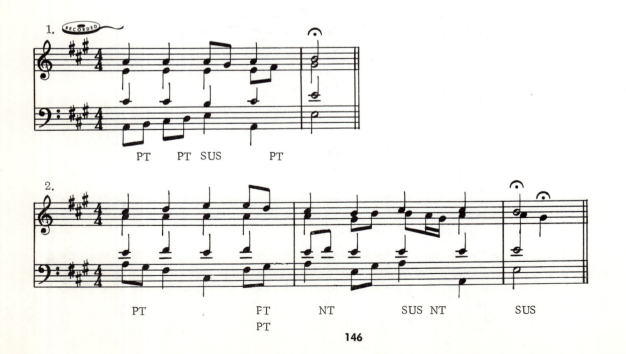

1. RECORDED

PT PT SUS PT

2.

PT FT NT SUS NT SUS
PT

146

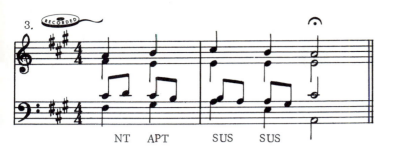

3.

NT   APT   SUS   SUS

4.

PT   PT   NT   ET   PT PT APT

5.

PT   SUS   SUS   ANT SUS   ET
PT   OR
                           DELAYED PT

6.

ET   APP   SUS   PT   ANT SUS
                             PT

Workbook Page 125

HARMONY UNIT NO. 9

B. ERRORS IN FOUR PART WRITING

To the Student: Below you see a series of four part exercises containing errors in the manuscript. The teacher will play the correct version.

Directions:

Numbers 1-10—Two chords only. The first chord is correct, but there is *one* error in the second chord of each exercise. Place a circle around the incorrect note.

Numbers 11-16—Each exercise consists of several chords, and contains 4, 5, or 6 errors. Place a circle around each incorrect note.

To the Teacher: Most of the exercises can be completed without playing the notes of the chords separately (rolling the chords). Play all notes of each chord simultaneously unless the majority of students cannot work the exercises in this manner.

*These circles indicate the notes which differ from those in the Student Workbook.

Workbook Page 127

HARMONY UNIT NO. 9

C. SOPRANO FACTORS, BASS FACTORS, CHORD QUALITY

To the Student: The teacher will play a series of chords.

Directions:
1. Write the soprano factor in the first set of blanks.
2. Write the bass factor in the second set of blanks.
3. Write the quality of chord: Major (M), Minor (m), diminished (D) in the third set of blanks.

To the Teacher: Emphasize the soprano voice the first time, the bass voice the second time, and maintain a balanced sound on the third playing.

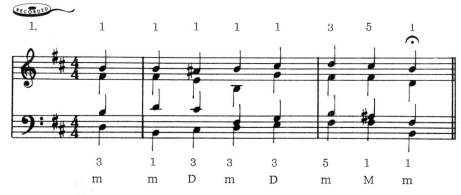

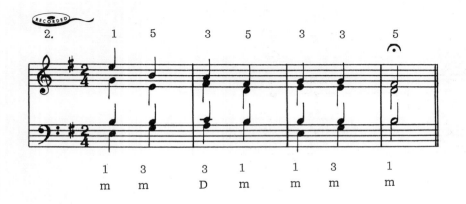

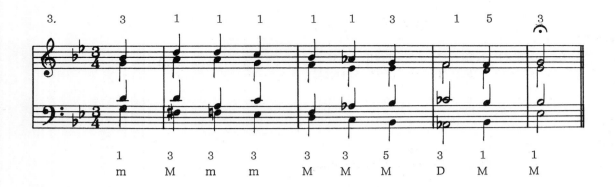

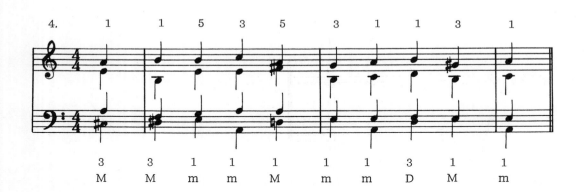

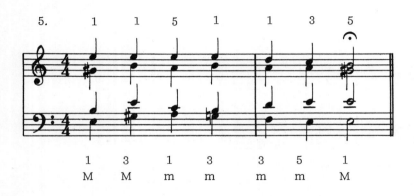

6.

5	1	3	5	3	3	3	5

1	3	1	3	1	3	5	1
m	M	m	M	M	m	M	M

HARMONY UNIT NO. 9

Workbook Page 128

D. RECOGNITION OF THE I, V, VII⁶, IV, AND II TRIAD
RECOGNITION OF THE MAJOR, MINOR, AND DIMINISHED TRIAD

To the Student: Each exercise consists of a phrase of music in four part harmony.

Directions:
1. Write the chord analysis in the blanks.
2. Write the coloration (quality) of the chord in the blanks.

To the Teacher:
1. Play once *very* slowly for chord analysis.
2. Play again for coloration (chord quality).

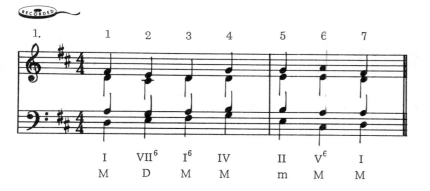

1.

1	2	3	4	5	6	7

I	VII⁶	I⁶	IV	II	Vᴱ	I
M	D	M	M	m	M	M

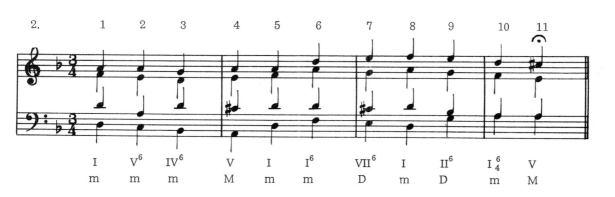

2.

1	2	3	4	5	6	7	8	9	10	11

I	V⁶	IV⁶	V	I	I⁶	VII⁶	I	II⁶	I⁶₄	V
m	m	m	M	m	m	D	m	D	m	M

151

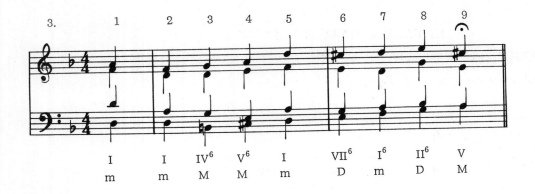

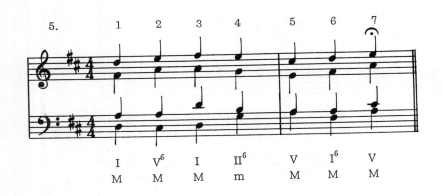

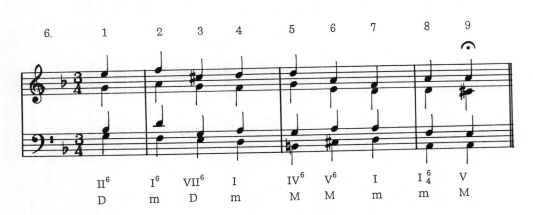

HARMONY UNIT NO. 10
A. RECOGNITION OF THE I, V, VII⁶, IV, II, AND V⁷ CHORD

To the Student: The following exercises lack soprano and bass voices. The instructor will play each phrase in four voices.

Directions:
1. Add the soprano voice on the staff.
2. Add the bass voice on the staff.
3. Make a Roman Numeral analysis including notation of inversions.

Optional for advanced students:
4. Add also the alto and tenor voices where they are not given.

To the Teacher:
1. Play once or twice emphasizing the soprano voice.
2. Play once or twice emphasizing the bass voice.
3. Play once or twice slowly for analysis.

---

*"×" indicates note is missing in Student Workbook.

HARMONY UNIT NO. 10

Workbook Page 131

B. BASS AND SOPRANO FACTORS

To the Student: Below are a series of incomplete Major-Minor Seventh Chords. The teacher will play the complete chords in four voices.

Directions:

Numbers 1 through 10:
 1. Place the number indicating the soprano factor in the blank.
 2. Write the soprano note on the staff.

Numbers 11 through 20:
 1. Place the number indicating the bass factor in the blank.
 2. Write the bass note on the staff.

Optional:

3. Write also the tenor note on the staff.

Numbers 21 through 30:

1. Place the number indicating the soprano factor in the blank.
2. Place the number indicating the bass factor in the blank.
3. Write the soprano note on the staff.

Optional:

4. Write the tenor and alto notes on the staff also.

Numbers 31 through 40:

1. Write the soprano factor numbers in the blanks.
2. Write the bass factor numbers in the blanks.
3. Write the soprano and bass notes on the staff.

To the Teacher: Play each chord two or three times stressing particular factors only if the students require it. Try to accustom the students to the sound of balanced voices.

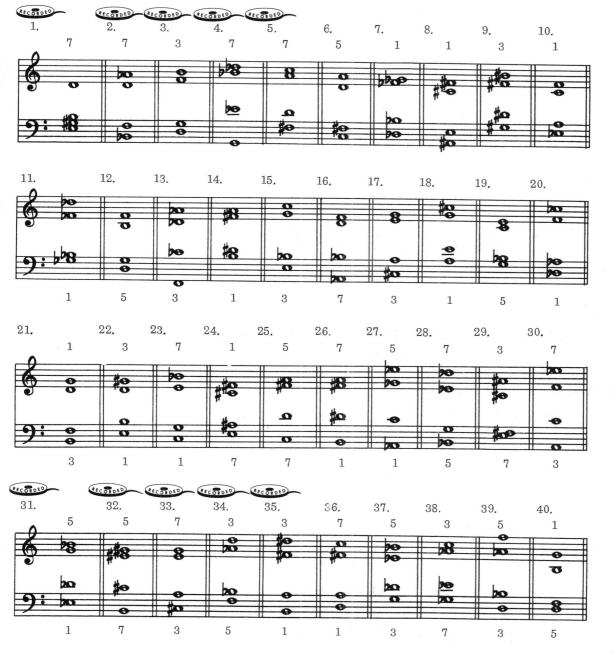

155

HARMONY UNIT NO. 10

C. CHORDS IN SCRAMBLED ORDER

To the Student: Each exercise consists of a phrase from a Bach Chorale played by the instructor. The chords are shown below, but are not in the proper order.

Directions: As the teacher plays the Chorale number the chords in the order they are played.

To the Teacher: Play the chords as written and slow enough for the student to search the scrambled order he has before him.

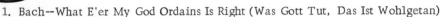

1. Bach--What E'er My God Ordains Is Right (Was Gott Tut, Das Ist Wohlgetan)

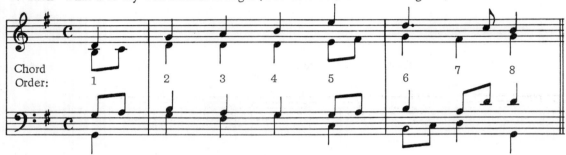

Student
Answer: 45218673

2. Bach--If Thou But Suffer God to Guide Thee (Wernur Den Lieben Gott Lasst Walten)

Student
Answer: 192837465

3. Bach--Lord, All My Heart Is Fixed on Thee (Herzlich Lief Ich Dich, O Herr)

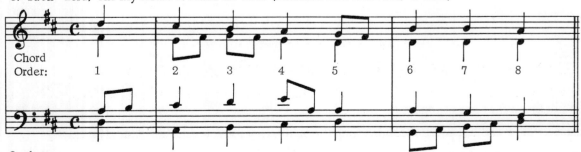

Student
Answer: 78235461

4. Bach--A Lamb Goes Forth (Lammlein Geht)

CHORD
ORDER: 1   2   3   4   5   6   7   8

Student
Answer: 52861374

5. Bach--Oh Eternity Holy Word (Oewigheit, Du Donnerwort)

CHORD
ORDER: 1   2   3   4   5   6   7   8

Student
Answer: 36187254

6. Bach--Our Father in Heaven (Vater Unser Im Himmelreich)

CHORD
ORDER: 1   2   3   4   5   6   7   8

Student
Answer: 48172653

Workbook Page 134

HARMONY UNIT NO. 10

D. IDENTIFICATION OF NON-HARMONIC DEVICES

To the Student: Each exercise consists of a two chord figure containing a non-harmonic tone. The instructor will play each for you.

Directions: Place the abbreviation indicating the non-harmonic tone in the blanks provided.

1. Unaccented passing tone   ___ U P T
2. Accented passing tone   ___ A P T

3. Suspension   __ S

4. Neighboring tone   __ N T

5. Appoggiatura   __ A

6. Escape tone   __ E T

7. Anticipation   __ A N T

To the Teacher: Play each exercise at an approximate speed of MM 60 per quarter note.

HARMONY UNIT NO. 11

A. RECOGNITION OF THE I, V, VII⁶, IV, II, V⁷ AND VI CHORD

To the Student: Each exercise consists of four possible chord progressions, Column 1, Column 2, Column 3, and Column 4. The instructor plays one of the four.

Directions: Circle the correct chord progression (in Column 1, Column 2, Column 3, or Column 4).

To the Teacher:
1. Play the tonic triad and have the students sing the I, V, VII, IV, II, V⁷, and VI chord. Call out various chords and have the student sing it immediately (1 - 3 - 5 - 3 - 1, or any system you prefer).
2. Play each exercise at an approximate speed of one chord per two seconds. Emphasize the bass slightly.

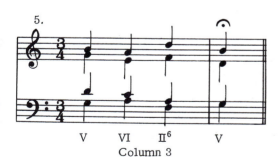

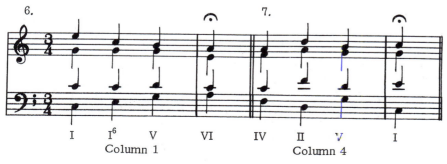

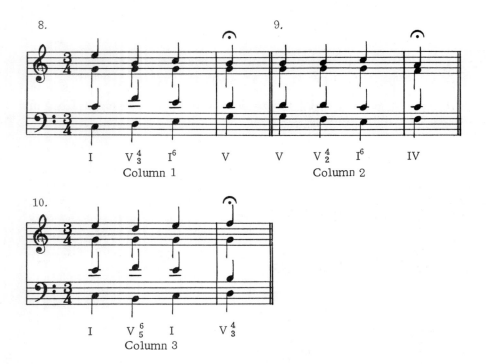

Column 1

Column 2

Column 3

Workbook Page 135

HARMONY UNIT NO. 11

B. RECOGNITION OF ERRORS IN FOUR PART WRITING

To the Student: Each of the following exercises contains errors in the manuscript. The instructor will play it correctly.

Directions: Place a circle around those notes that are different from those played by the instructor.

To the Teacher: Play each exercise at a speed of one chord per two seconds. Do not "roll" (arpeggiate) the chords.

---

*These circles indicate the notes which differ from those in the Student Workbook.

HARMONY UNIT NO. 11

C. RECOGNITION OF BACKGROUND HARMONY

To the Student: Each exercise is a melody with background accompaniment. The melody is printed for you.

Directions: Write the analysis of the background accompaniment in the blanks provided. The chords will be one of the following: I, V, VII, IV, II, or VI—do not try to figure out the inversions. Optional for advanced students—include also the inversions.

To the Teacher: Experiment by playing these compositions at their normal tempo. If the students fail to comprehend the background harmonies, then slow them down until the student can be accommodated.

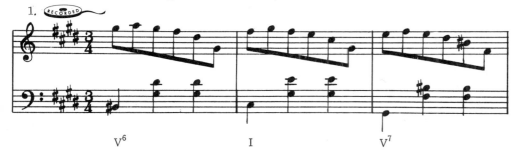

VI Neapolitan None

V⁷ I

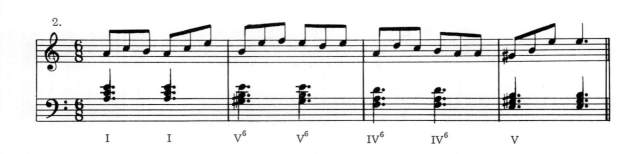

2.

I I V⁶ V⁶ IV⁶ IV⁶ V

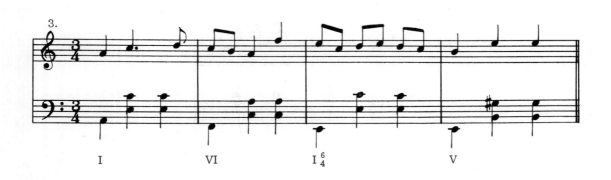

3.

I VI I$^6_4$ V

4.

I V II

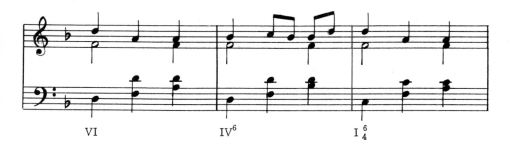

VI   IV^6 I $^6_4$

V^7

5.

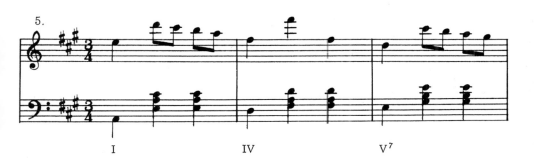

I   IV   V^7

I^6 I   IV^6

V^7 I

I   VI⁶   IV⁶   V⁶   I

IV⁶   V   I

Workbook Page 138

HARMONY UNIT NO. 11

D. BASS FACTORS, SOPRANO FACTORS, CHORD QUALITY

To the Student: Following is a series of isolated notes. These represent the bass notes of chords. The teacher plays the entire chord.

Directions:
1. Write the soprano factor in the space above the staff.
2. Write the bass factor in the space below the staff.
3. Write the soprano note on the staff in notation.
4. Indicate whether the chord is Major (M), Minor (m), Diminished (D), or Major-Minor seventh (Mm) in the second row of blanks beneath the bass note.

Optional:
5. Write *all* missing notes of the chord on the staff.

To the Teacher: Play each chord slowly and simultaneously emphasizing either bass and soprano only if absolutely necessary. For drill students may still sing the chord in simple root position immediately after it is played. Emphasis should now be on speed, and the earlier aids to perception should be gradually discontinued.

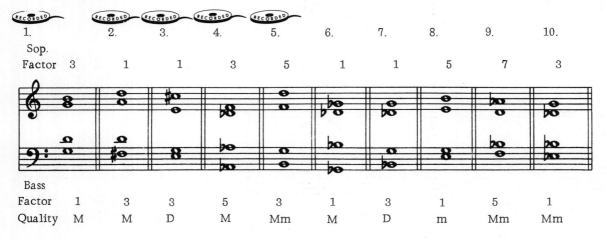

	1.	2.	3.	4.	5.	6.	7.	8.	9.	10.
Sop. Factor	3	1	1	3	5	1	1	5	7	3
Bass Factor	1	3	3	5	3	1	3	1	5	1
Quality	M	M	D	M	Mm	M	D	m	Mm	Mm

164

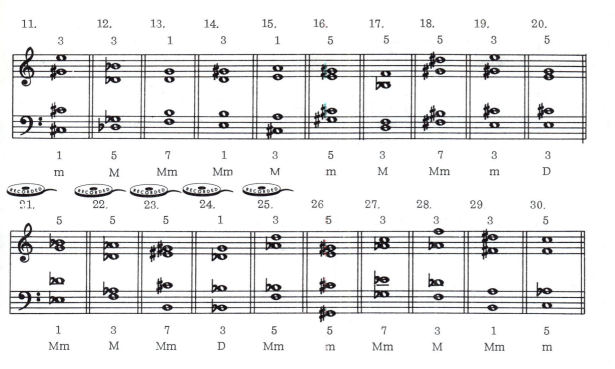

Workbook Page 139

HARMONY UNIT NO. 12

A. RECOGNITION OF THE I, V, VII⁶, IV, II, V⁷, AND III TRIADS

To the Student: One voice of a four part harmonization is missing. The instructor will play all four voices.

Directions:
1. Add the missing voice to the staff.
2. Make a complete harmonic analysis.

To the Teacher: Play each exercise at an approximate speed of one chord per two seconds.

1. All Soprano (Except First Note) Is Missing in Student Workbook

2. All Bass (Except First Note) Is Missing in Student Workbook

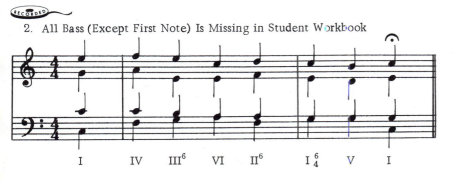

165

3. All Soprano (Except First Note) Is Missing in Student Workbook

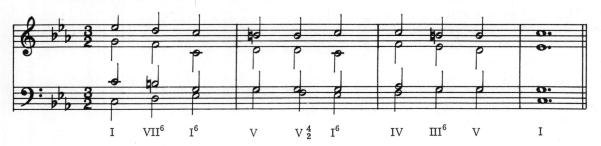

I   VII⁶   I⁶   V   V $\frac{4}{2}$ I⁶   IV   III⁶   V   I

4. All Bass (Except First Note) Is Missing in Student Workbook

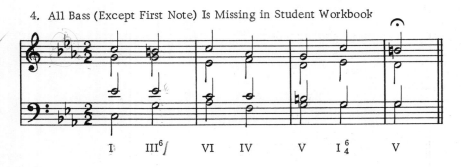

I   III⁶   VI   IV   V   I $\frac{6}{4}$ V

5. All Bass (Except First Note) Is Missing in Student Workbook

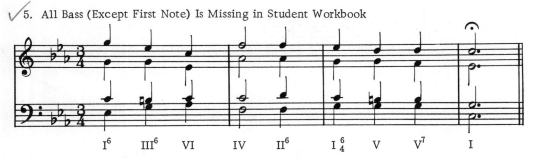

I⁶   III⁶   VI   IV   II⁶   I $\frac{6}{4}$ V   V⁷   I

6. All Soprano (Except First Note) Is Missing in Student Workbook

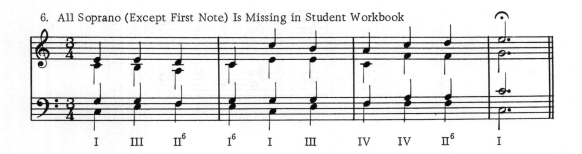

I   III   II⁶   I⁶   I   III   IV   IV   II⁶   I

Workbook Page 140   **HARMONY UNIT NO. 12**

B. SOPRANO FACTORS, BASS FACTORS, CHORD QUALITY

To the Student: Following is a series of isolated notes. These represent voices of four-part major, minor, diminished triads, and Major-Minor Seventh chords. The teacher plays the complete chord.

Directions:
Numbers 1-10: BASS NOTE GIVEN
     1. Write the soprano factor.
     2. Write the bass factor.

3. Write the soprano note.
4. Write the chord quality.

Numbers 11-20: SOPRANO NOTE GIVEN
1. Write the soprano factor.
2. Write the bass factor.
3. Write the bass note.
4. Write the chord quality.

Numbers 21-30: ALTO AND TENOR NOTES GIVEN
1. Write the soprano note.
2. Write the bass note.

Optional on all exercises:
   Write *all* missing voices on the staff in notation.
When you hear an augmented triad simply place an "A" in all blanks.

To the Teacher: Play each chord slowly and all notes simultaneously emphasizing particular voices only if absolutely necessary.

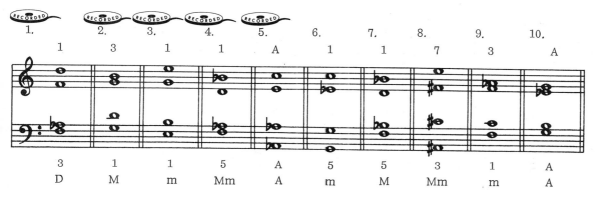

167

HARMONY UNIT NO. 12
C. IDENTIFICATION OF NON-HARMONIC DEVICES

To the Student: Each exercise consists of a two chord figure containing a non-harmonic tone. The instructor will play each for you.

Directions: Place the abbreviation indicating the non-harmonic tone in the blanks provided.

1. Unaccented passing tone   ___ U P T
2. Accented passing tone   ___ A P T
3. Suspension   ___ S
4. Neighboring tone   ___ N T
5. Appoggiatura   ___ A
6. Escape tone   ___ E T
7. Anticipation   ___ A N T

To the Teacher: Play each exercise at an approximate speed of MM 60 per quarter note.

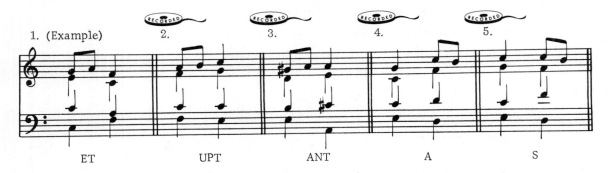

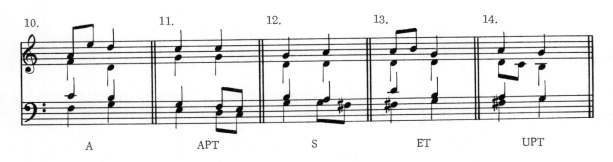

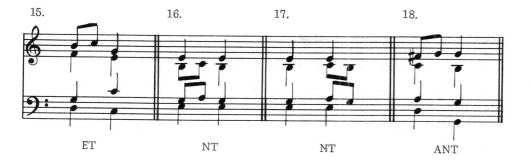

ET   NT   NT   ANT

HARMONY UNIT NO. 12
D. RECOGNITION OF THE III TRIAD

To the Student: Each exercise is a short series of four part chords. *One* of the chords in each exercise is a III triad. Each blank below represents a chord played by the instructor.

Directions: Write "III" in the blank where you hear a mediant (III) triad.
Optional: Make a complete harmonic analysis of all chords played.

To the Teacher: Play each exercise at an approximate speed of MM 60 per quarter note.

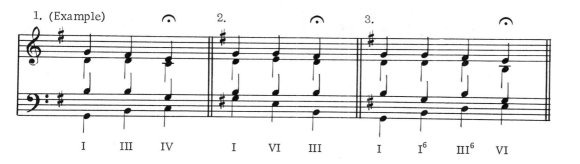

1. (Example)   I   III   IV   2. I   VI   III   3. I   I⁶   III⁶   VI

4. I   V   VI   III   5. I   III⁶   VI   IV   V

6. III   I   V   VI

7.

II   V⁷   I   III

8.

I   VI   III⁶   V

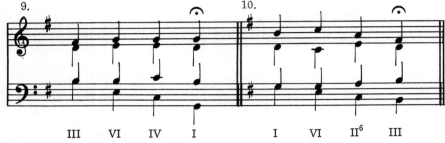

9.

III   VI   IV   I

10.

I   VI   II⁶   III

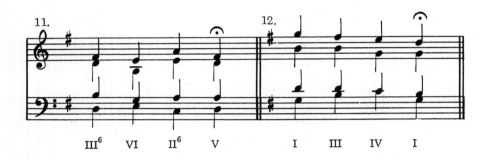

11.

III⁶   VI   II⁶   V

12.

I   III   IV   I

Workbook Page 143

HARMONY UNIT NO. 13

A. RECOGNITION OF MODULATION TO THE DOMINANT, SUBDOMINANT, AND RELATIVE MINOR

To the Student: Each exercise modulates either to the dominant, subdominant, or relative minor key. The first chord is always the tonic chord in the original key.

Directions: Indicate the modulation by writing "Dominant," "Subdominant," or "Relative Minor" in the blanks below.
Optional for advanced students: Beside the answer requested above include also a complete analysis of each chord played including the point of modulation.

To the Teacher: Play each exercise at an approximate speed of one chord per two or three seconds.

1. Answer--Relative Minor

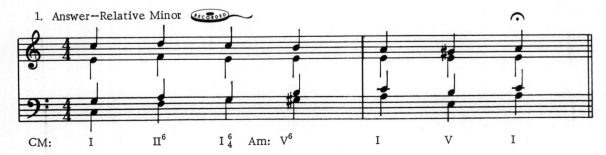

CM: I   II⁶   I $^6_4$ Am: V⁶   I   V   I

8. Answer--Subdominant

DM: I   IV⁶   V   I

GM: { IV I   V   I

9. Answer--Relative Minor

DM: I VII⁶ I⁶   IV V V   VI { VI

Bm: { I   V   I

10. Answer--Dominant

DM: I   V⁶   I   VI   III   { VI⁶

AM: { II⁶   V   I

11. Answer--Subdominant

DM: I   V   VI   II⁶   V   I⁶   { IV

GM: { I   II   V   I

12. Answer--Dominant

DM: I   III   IV   { V

AM: { I   V   V⁷   I

172

HARMONY UNIT NO. 13
B. DICTATION OF MODULATING EXERCISES USING HARMONIC LANGUAGE STUDIED TO DATE

To the Student: Each exercise modulates.

Directions:
1. Add the soprano voice to the staff.
2. Add the bass voice to the staff.
3. Make a complete harmonic analysis.

Optional:
4. Add the alto and tenor voice also to the staff.

To the Teacher: Play each exercise at an approximate speed of one chord per two or three seconds. Generally three playing are sufficient—(1) Emphasize the soprano (2) Emphasize the bass (3) play the chords balanced for harmonic analysis.

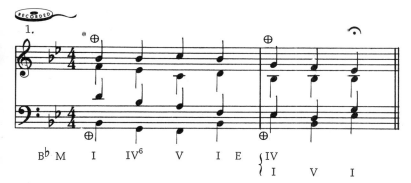

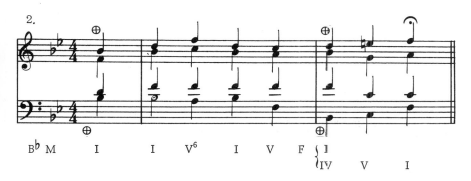

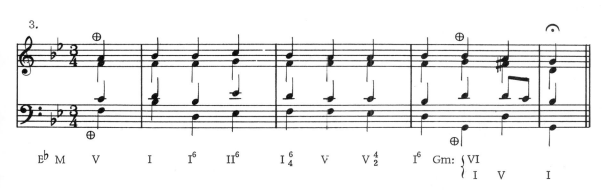

---

* ⊕ indicates note is given in Student Workbook.

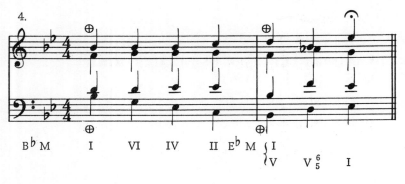

4.

B♭M   I   VI   IV   II   E♭M { I
   V   V $\frac{6}{5}$ I

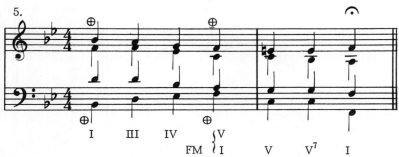

5.

I   III   IV   { V
FM { I   V   V^7 I

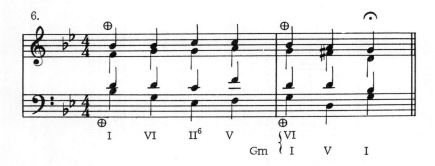

6.

I   VI   II^6 V   { VI
Gm { I   V   I

Workbook Page 145

HARMONY UNIT NO. 13

C. RECOGNITION OF AUTHENTIC, HALF, PLAGAL, AND DECEPTIVE CADENCES IN NON-MODULATING EXERCISES

To the Student: Each exercise ends with one of the following cadences:

AUTHENTIC	HALF	PLAGAL	DECEPTIVE
V to I, V^7 to I, VII^6 to I	I to V, II to V, VI to V	IV to I	V to VI, V^7 to VI

Directions: Determine which type of cadence is used, and write the name of it in the proper blank below. Optional for advanced students: Write also the analysis of all the chords in each exercise.

To the Teacher: Play each exercise at an approximate speed of one chord per two seconds. Generally students will need only one hearing, but slower students may require two or three.

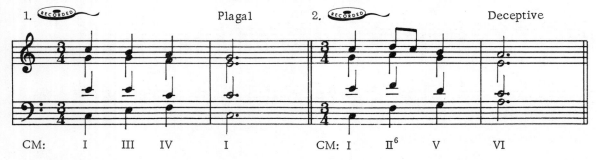

1. (RECORDED)   Plagal   2. (RECORDED)   Deceptive

CM: I   III   IV   I   CM: I   II^6 V   VI

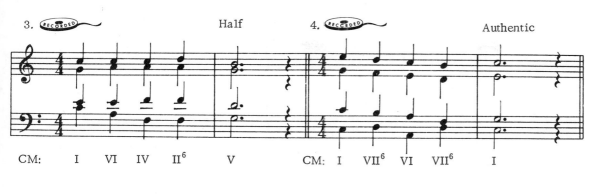

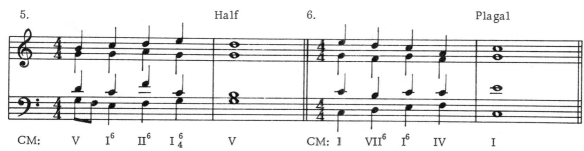

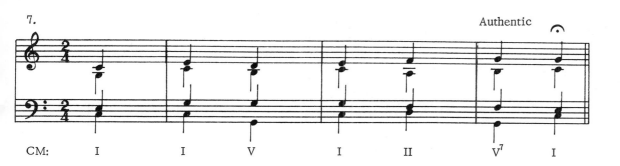

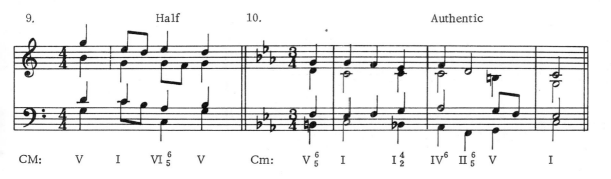

11.

Half

Cm: V⁶ I V⁴₃ I⁶ II⁶ I⁶₄ I V

12.

Deceptive

Cm: V⁴₃ I VI II⁶₅ VII⁷ of V V V⁷ VI

13.

Half

I IV⁶ II⁶ V

14.

Deceptive

I IV V VI

15.

Plagal

I I⁶ IV I

16.

Authentic

IV⁷ I⁶₄ V I

17.

Authentic

IV IV V⁷ I

18.

Deceptive

IV IV⁷ V VI

176

HARMONY UNIT NO. 13

D. EASIER, NON-MODULATING EXERCISES FOR SPEED IN DICTATING

To the Student: These exercises are especially designed for speed in dictation.

Directions:
1. Write the soprano melody on the staff.
2. Write the bass melody on the staff.
3. Make a complete harmonic analysis.
   Option for advanced students:
4. Write the alto and tenor also on the staff.

To the Teacher: Experiment with speeds of MM 44 to 60 per second. Most students by this time will be capable of this faster speed. Generally two or three playings will be sufficient.
First bass and soprano note given in Student Workbook.

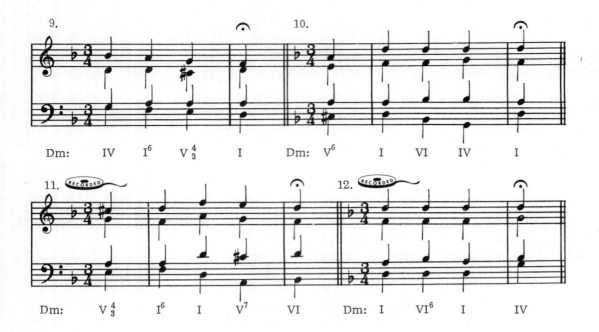

9.

10.

Dm: IV   I⁶   V 4/3   I   Dm: V⁶   I   VI   IV   I

11. RECORDED

12. RECORDED

Dm: V 4/3   I⁶   I   V⁷   VI   Dm: I   VI⁶   I   IV

Workbook Page 148

HARMONY UNIT NO. 14

A. RECOGNITION OF THE I, V, VII⁶, IV, II, V⁷, VI AND III CHORDS

To the Student: Two short harmonic exercises will be played—one immediately following the other. Listen for the BASIC chord structure in each. Different arrangements and inversions of the same chord still produce the same BASIC chord structure.

Directions:
1. Mark SAME in the blank if the Roman Numeral analysis of the two short phrases is the same. Disregard inversions and arrangements of the same chord.
2. Mark DIFFERENT in the blank if the Roman Numeral analysis of the two short phrases is different.

To the Teacher: Play the first set of progressions, pause slightly, then play the second set (1a then 1b). A speed of approximately two seconds per chord is suggested. If students have difficulty with this have them sing each chord in each section in simple (three note chord in root position) position.

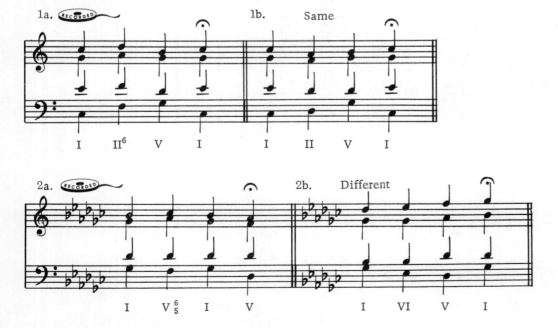

1a. RECORDED   1b.   Same

I   II⁶   V   I   I   II   V   I

2a. RECORDED   2b.   Different

I   V 6/5   I   V   I   VI   V   I

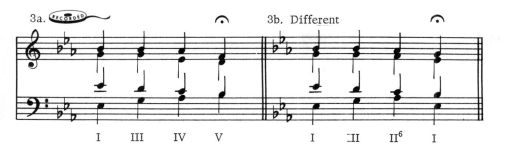

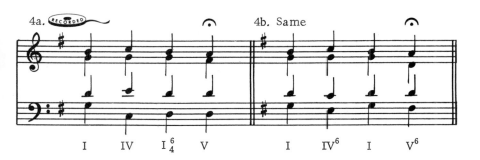

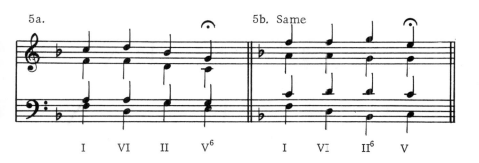

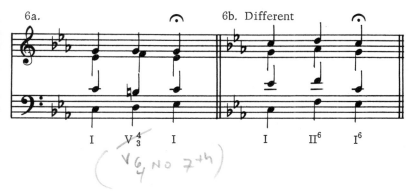

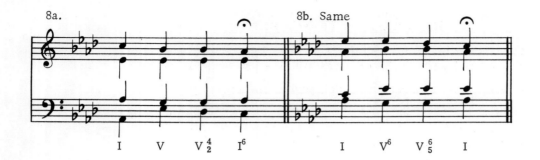

8a.

I V V$^4_2$ I^6

8b. Same

I V^6 V$^6_5$ I

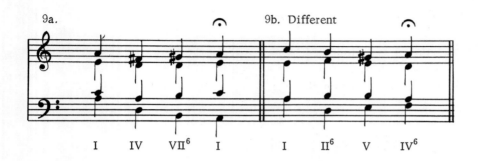

9a.

I IV VII^6 I

9b. Different

I II^6 V IV^6

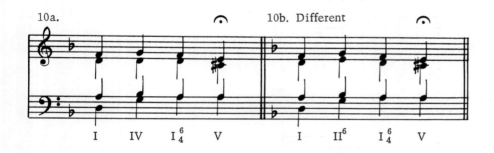

10a.

I IV I$^6_4$ V

10b. Different

I II^6 I$^6_4$ V

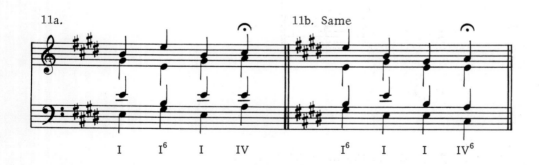

11a.

I I^6 I IV

11b. Same

I^6 I I IV^6

12a.

V V$^4_3$ I V

12b. Same

V V$^4_2$ I^6 V

180

B. DICTATION OF MODULATING EXERCISES
USING ALL DIATONIC TRIADS AND THE V⁷ CHORD

To the Student: Each exercise consists of a short harmonic phrase in four voices.

Directions:
1. Add the soprano line to the staff.
2. Add the bass line to the staff.
3. Make a complete harmonic analysis.
Optional for advanced students:
4. Write also the alto and tenor voice on the staff.

To the Teacher:
1. Play once or twice emphasizing the soprano line.
2. Play once or twice emphasizing the bass line.
3. Play again once or twice (slower) for analysis—about one chord per two or three seconds.

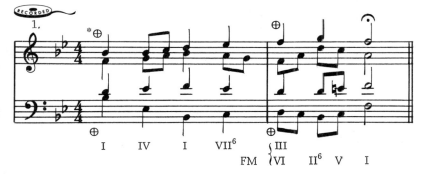

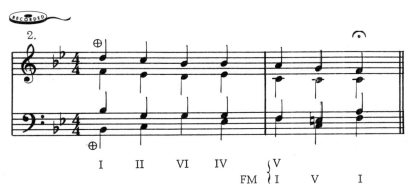

---

* ⊕ indicates note is given in Student Workbook.

181

4.

I   I   II⁶   II   V⁶₅   I   IV   {IV⁶ / I⁶}   V⁷   I

E♭ M

5.

I   I⁶   V   I   {I / VI}   V⁶   V   I

D♭ M

6.

I   III   IV   V⁶₅   I   {III / IV}   V   I

A♭ M

Workbook Page 150

HARMONY UNIT NO. 14

C. ERRORS IN DICTATED PIECES OF DIFFERENT TEXTURES

To the Student: In the following short excerpts the music you see before you is correct. When the instructor plays these he will make THREE ERRORS PER EXERCISE.

    Directions: Place a circle around those notes which have been incorrectly played.

To the Teacher: Play the exercise over at its normal speed.

1.

Etc.

———————

*Circles indicate notes which disagree with notes in Student Notebooks.

Workbook Page 152

HARMONY UNIT NO. 14

D. RECOGNITION OF MODULATION TO ALL FIVE CLOSELY RELATED KEYS

To the Student: Each exercise modulates to one of the five closely related keys.

Directions: Write the KEY and MODE (major or minor) to which the exercise modulates. Optional for advanced students—Also provide a complete harmonic analysis of all chords.

CLOSELY RELATED KEYS TO A *MAJOR* KEY—
Dominant Major
Subdominant Major   all have
Supertonic Minor   1. the same signature, or
Mediant Minor   2. one sharp (flat) more, or
Submediant Minor   3. one sharp (flat) less.

CLOSELY RELATED KEYS TO A *MINOR* KEY—
Dominant Minor   all have
Mediant Major
Subtonic Major   1. the same signature, or
Subdominant Minor   2. one sharp (flat) more, or
Submediant Major   3. one sharp (flat) less.

To the Teacher: Play each exercise at an approximate speed of one chord per two seconds. If students have difficulty have them sing the tonic at the beginning of the exercise and hold it (out loud) until the final cadence is played in the new key; then, skip immediately to the new tonic. Then, have them sing the old and the new several times until they have determined the relationship.

1. CM to Am

CM: I   I⁶   V   Am: V⁶   I   V   I

184

CM to Dm

2. RECORDED

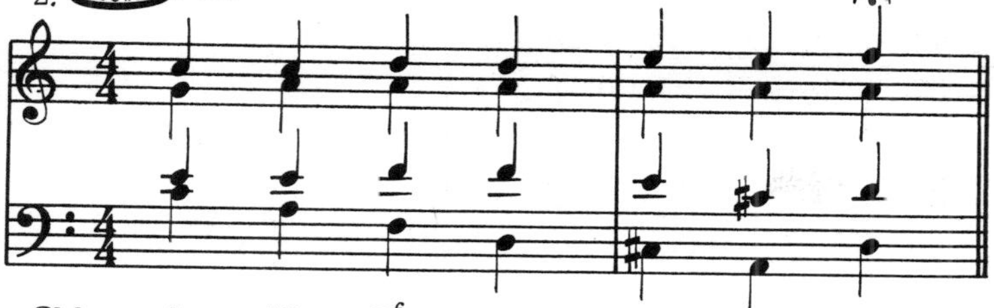

CM: I VI II^6 {II
Dm {I V^6 V I

CM to Em

3. RECORDED

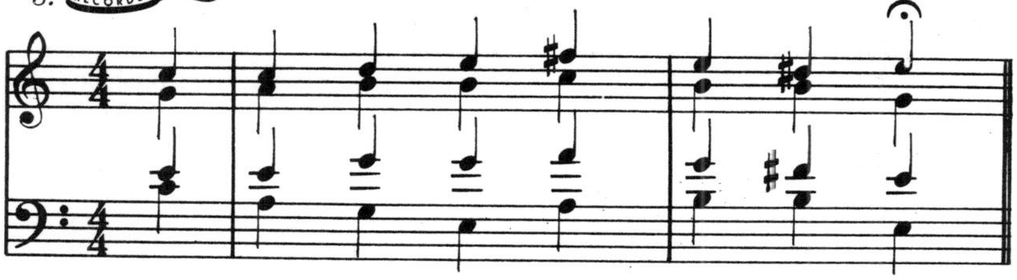

CM: I VI V {III
Em {I II^6 I$^6_4$ V I

CM to GM

4.

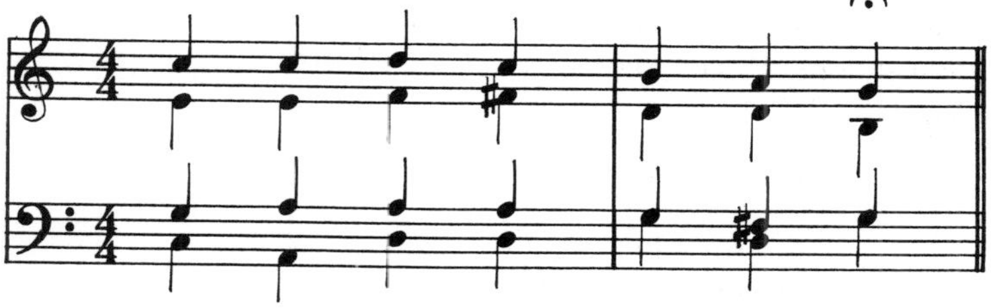

CM: I VI II GM V^7 I V I

CM to Am

5.

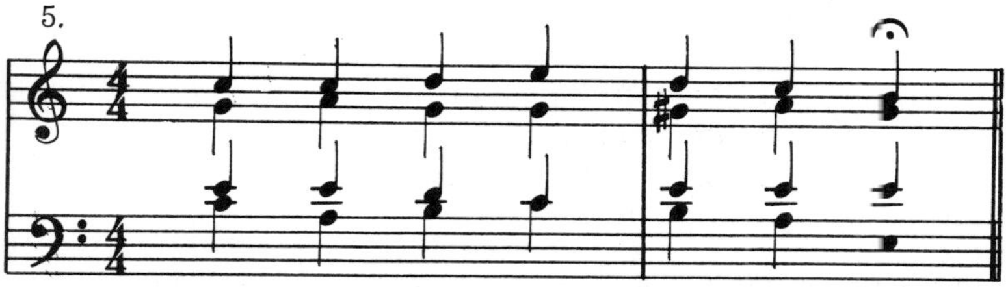

CM I VI V^6 I Am V$^4_3$ I V

Cm to E^{b}M

6.

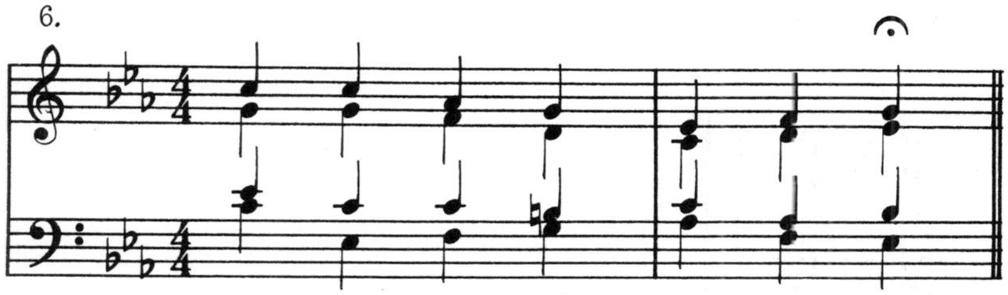

Cm I I^6 IV V {VI
E^{b}M {IV VII^3 I

Cm to A♭M

7.

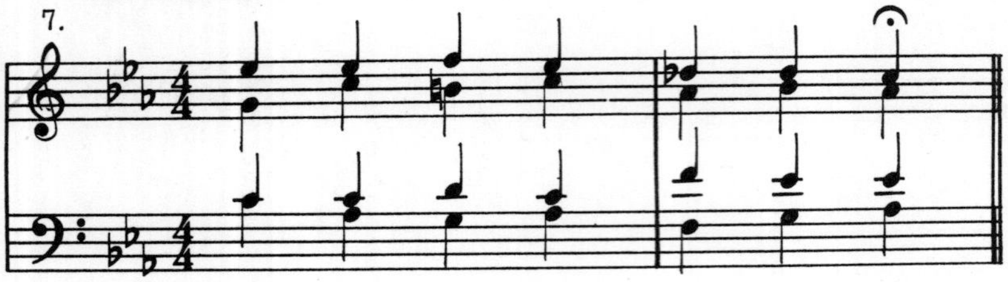

Cm I VI V^7 {VI
A♭M {I IV^6 V^6_5 I

Workbook Page 153

HARMONY UNIT NO. 15

A. RECOGNITION OF MAJOR, MINOR, AUGMENTED, AND DIMINISHED TRIADS

To the Student: The instructor will play four triads in succession—one major, one minor, one diminished, and one augmented.

Directions: Write the order in which these triads are played. Use:

Major—M Minor—m Diminished—D Augmented—A

To the Teacher: Play each set of triads at a speed of about MM 60. This is an exercise designed to encourage quick perception.

1. (example)

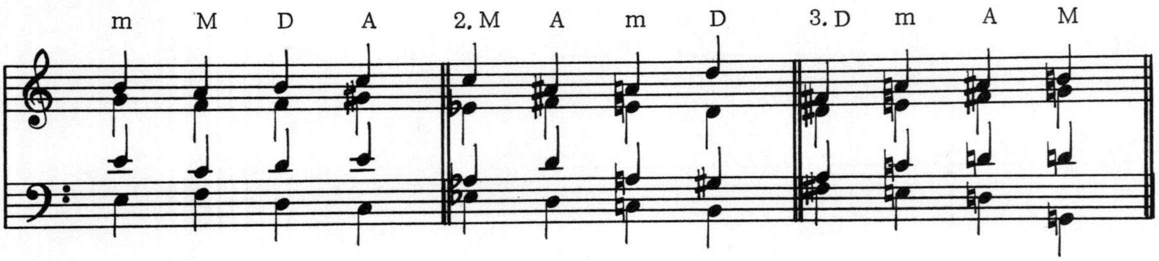
m M D A
2. M A m D
3. D m A M

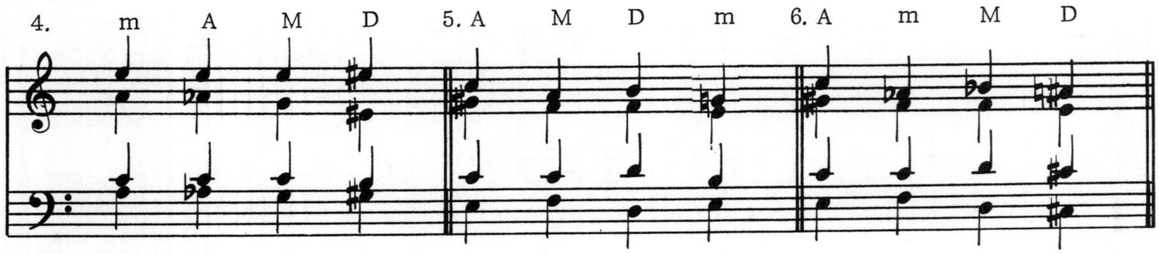
4. m A M D
5. A M D m
6. A m M D

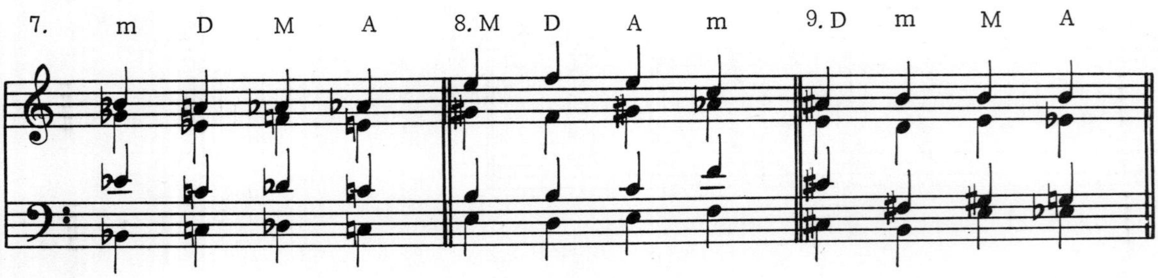
7. m D M A
8. M D A m
9. D m M A

8. Answer--Subdominant

DM: I   IV^6 V   I

GM: { IV / I   V   I

9. Answer--Relative Minor

DM: I   VII^6 I^6 IV   V   V   VI

Bm: { VI / I   V   I

10. Answer--Dominant

DM: I   V^6 I   VI   III

AM: { VI^6 / II^6 V   I

11. Answer--Subdominant

DM: I   V   VI   II^6 V   I^6

GM: { IV / I   II   V   I

12. Answer--Dominant

DM: I   III   IV

AM: { V / I   V   V^7 I

HARMONY UNIT NO. 13

B. DICTATION OF MODULATING EXERCISES USING HARMONIC LANGUAGE STUDIED TO DATE

To the Student: Each exercise modulates.

Directions:
1. Add the soprano voice to the staff.
2. Add the bass voice to the staff.
3. Make a complete harmonic analysis.

Optional:
4. Add the alto and tenor voice also to the staff.

To the Teacher: Play each exercise at an approximate speed of one chord per two or three seconds. Generally three playing are sufficient—(1) Emphasize the soprano (2) Emphasize the bass (3) play the chords balanced for harmonic analysis.

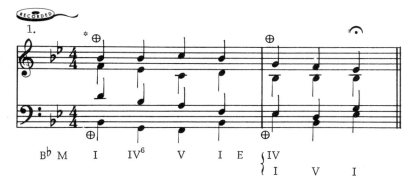

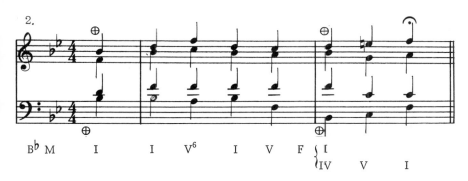

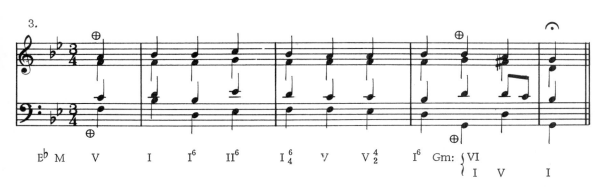

* ⊕ indicates note is given in Student Workbook.

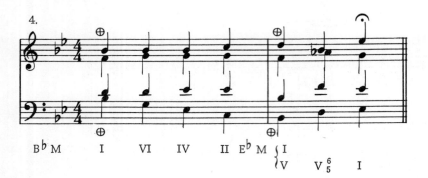

4.

B^b M   I   VI   IV   II E^b M { I / V V^6_5 I }

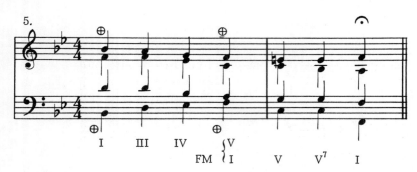

5.

I   III   IV   FM { V / I }   V V^7 I

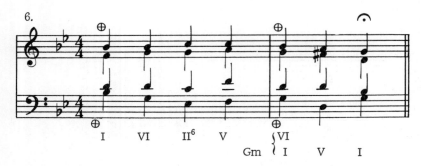

6.

I   VI II^6 V   Gm { VI / I }   V   I

Workbook Page 145

HARMONY UNIT NO. 13

C. RECOGNITION OF AUTHENTIC, HALF, PLAGAL, AND DECEPTIVE CADENCES IN NON-MODULATING EXERCISES

To the Student: Each exercise ends with one of the following cadences:

AUTHENTIC	HALF	PLAGAL	DECEPTIVE
V to I, V^7 to I, VII^6 to I	I to V, II to V, VI to V	IV to I	V to VI, V^7 to VI

Directions: Determine which type of cadence is used, and write the name of it in the proper blank below. Optional for advanced students: Write also the analysis of all the chords in each exercise.

To the Teacher: Play each exercise at an approximate speed of one chord per two seconds. Generally students will need only one hearing, but slower students may require two or three.

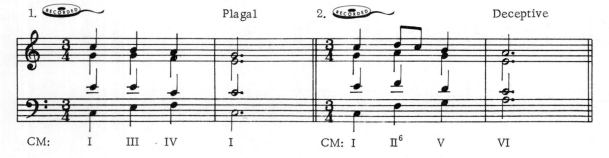

1. RECORDED   Plagal   2. RECORDED   Deceptive

CM: I   III   IV   I   CM: I II^6 V   VI

3. Half

CM: I   VI   IV   II⁶   V

4. Authentic

CM: I   VII⁶   VI   VII⁶   I

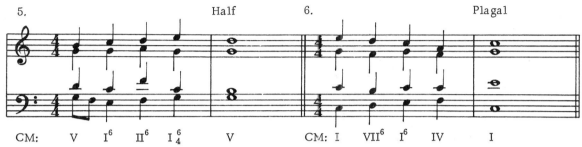

5. Half

CM: V   I⁶   II⁶   I⁶₄   V

6. Plagal

CM: I   VII⁶   I⁶   IV   I

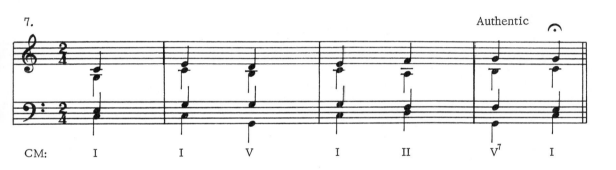

7. Authentic

CM: I   I   V   I   II   V⁷   I

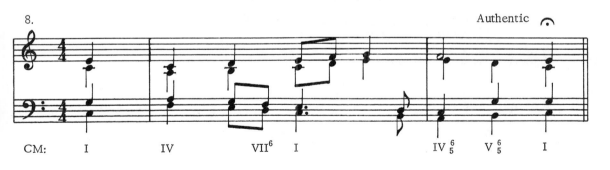

8. Authentic

CM: I   IV   VII⁶   I   IV⁶₅   V⁶₅   I

9. Half

CM: V   I   VI⁶₅   V

10. Authentic

Cm: V⁶₅   I   I⁴₂   IV⁶   II⁶₅   V   I

176

HARMONY UNIT NO. 13

D. EASIER, NON-MODULATING EXERCISES FOR SPEED IN DICTATING

To the Student: These exercises are especially designed for speed in dictation.

Directions:
1. Write the soprano melody on the staff.
2. Write the bass melody on the staff.
3. Make a complete harmonic analysis.
   Option for advanced students:
4. Write the alto and tenor also on the staff.

To the Teacher: Experiment with speeds of MM 44 to 60 per second. Most students by this time will be capable of this faster speed. Generally two or three playings will be sufficient.
First bass and soprano note given in Student Workbook.

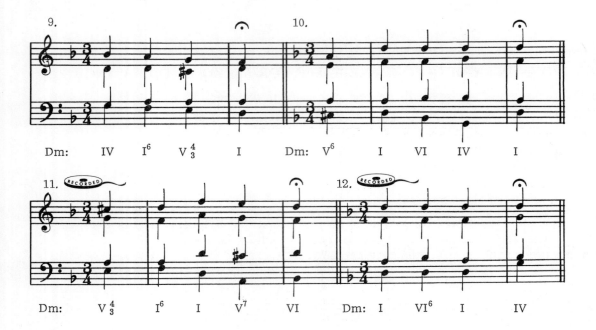

9. 10.

Dm: IV   I⁶   V⁴₃   I   Dm: V⁶   I   VI   IV   I

11. RECORDED   12. RECORDED

Dm: V⁴₃   I⁶   I   V⁷   VI   Dm: I   VI⁶   I   IV

Workbook Page 148

HARMONY UNIT NO. 14

A. RECOGNITION OF THE I, V, VII⁶, IV, II, V⁷, VI AND III CHORDS

To the Student: Two short harmonic exercises will be played—one immediately following the other. Listen for the BASIC chord structure in each. Different arrangements and inversions of the same chord still produce the same BASIC chord structure.

Directions:
1. Mark SAME in the blank if the Roman Numeral analysis of the two short phrases is the same. Disregard inversions and arrangements of the same chord.
2. Mark DIFFERENT in the blank if the Roman Numeral analysis of the two short phrases is different.

To the Teacher: Play the first set of progressions, pause slightly, then play the second set (1a then 1b). A speed of approximately two seconds per chord is suggested. If students have difficulty with this have them sing each chord in each section in simple (three note chord in root position) position.

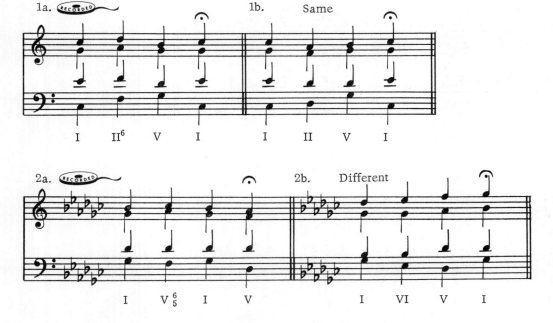

1a. RECORDED   1b.   Same

I   II⁶   V   I   I   II   V   I

2a. RECORDED   2b.   Different

I   V⁶₅   I   V   I   VI   V   I

178

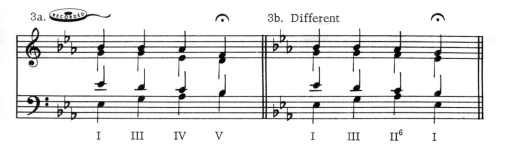

3a. RECORDED   3b. Different

I   III   IV   V   I   III   II⁶   I

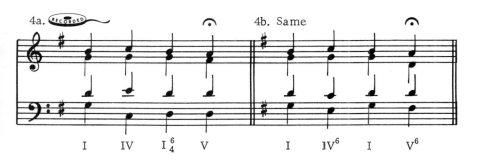

4a. RECORDED   4b. Same

I   IV   I$^6_4$ V   I   IV⁶   I   V⁶

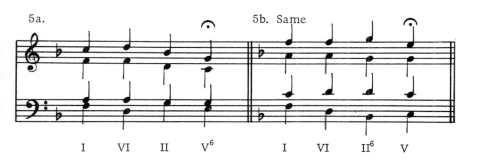

5a.   5b. Same

I   VI   II   V⁶   I   VI   II⁶   V

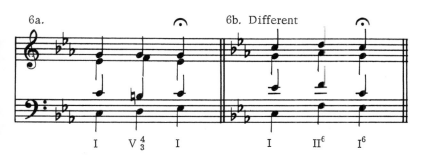

6a.   6b. Different

I   V$^4_3$ I   I   II⁶   I⁶

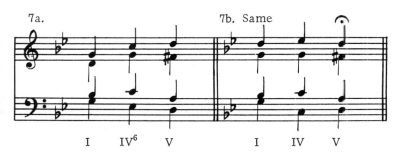

7a.   7b. Same

I   IV⁶   V   I   IV   V

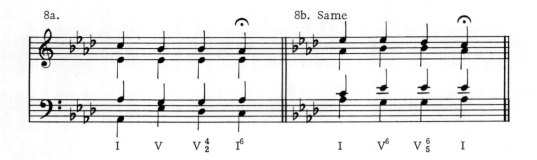

8a.

8b. Same

I   V   V $\frac{4}{2}$ I^6 I   V^6 V $\frac{6}{5}$ I

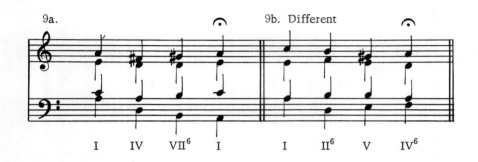

9a.

9b. Different

I   IV   VII^6 I   I   II^6 V   IV^6

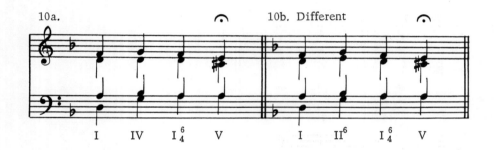

10a.

10b. Different

I   IV   I $\frac{6}{4}$ V   I   II^6 I $\frac{6}{4}$ V

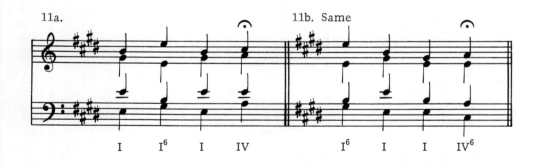

11a.

11b. Same

I   I^6 I   IV   I^6 I   I   IV^6

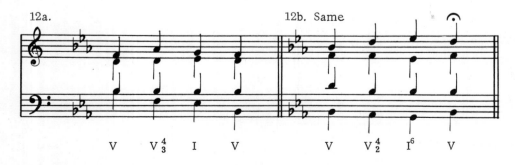

12a.

12b. Same

V   V $\frac{4}{3}$ I   V   V   V $\frac{4}{2}$ I^6 V

HARMONY UNIT NO. 14

B. DICTATION OF MODULATING EXERCISES
USING ALL DIATONIC TRIADS AND THE V⁷ CHORD

To the Student: Each exercise consists of a short harmonic phrase in four voices.

Directions:
1. Add the soprano line to the staff.
2. Add the bass line to the staff.
3. Make a complete harmonic analysis.

Optional for advanced students:
4. Write also the alto and tenor voice on the staff.

To the Teacher:
1. Play once or twice emphasizing the soprano line.
2. Play once or twice emphasizing the bass line.
3. Play again once or twice (slower) for analysis—about one chord per two or three seconds.

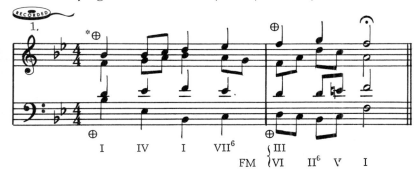

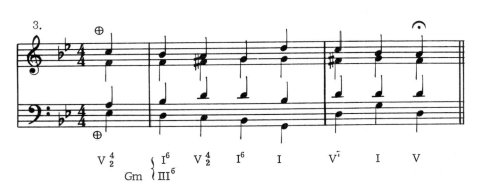

_____

* ⊕ indicates note is given in Student Workbook.

4.

I   I   II^6 II   V$^6_5$ I   IV $\left\{\begin{matrix}\text{IV}^6\\\text{I}^6\end{matrix}\right.$ V^7 I

                             E^{b}M

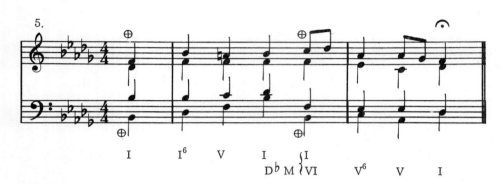

5.

I   I^6 V   I $\left\{\begin{matrix}\text{I}\\\text{VI}\end{matrix}\right.$ V^6 V I

                  D^{b}M

6.

I   III   IV   V$^6_5$ I $\left\{\begin{matrix}\text{III}\\\text{IV}\end{matrix}\right.$ V I

                        A^{b}M

Workbook Page 150

HARMONY UNIT NO. 14

C. ERRORS IN DICTATED PIECES OF DIFFERENT TEXTURES

To the Student: In the following short excerpts the music you see before you is correct. When the instructor plays these he will make THREE ERRORS PER EXERCISE.

    Directions: Place a circle around those notes which have been incorrectly played.

To the Teacher: Play the exercise over at its normal speed.

1.

Etc.

---

*Circles indicate notes which disagree with notes in Student Notebooks.

Etc.

Etc.

Etc.

Etc.

7.

Etc.

8.

HARMONY UNIT NO. 14
Workbook Page 152
D. RECOGNITION OF MODULATION TO ALL FIVE CLOSELY RELATED KEYS

To the Student: Each exercise modulates to one of the five closely related keys.

Directions: Write the KEY and MODE (major or minor) to which the exercise modulates. Optional for advanced students—Also provide a complete harmonic analysis of all chords.

CLOSELY RELATED KEYS TO A *MAJOR* KEY—

Dominant Major	all have
Subdominant Major	
Supertonic Minor	1. the same signature, or
Mediant Minor	2. one sharp (flat) more, or
Submediant Minor	3. one sharp (flat) less.

CLOSELY RELATED KEYS TO A *MINOR* KEY—

Dominant Minor	all have
Mediant Major	
Subtonic Major	1. the same signature, or
Subdominant Minor	2. one sharp (flat) more, or
Submediant Major	3. one sharp (flat) less.

To the Teacher: Play each exercise at an approximate speed of one chord per two seconds. If students have difficulty have them sing the tonic at the beginning of the exercise and hold it (out loud) until the final cadence is played in the new key; then, skip immediately to the new tonic. Then, have them sing the old and the new several times until they have determined the relationship.

1. CM to Am

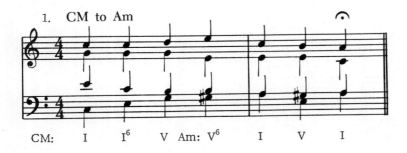

CM: I   I⁶   V   Am: V⁶   I   V   I

184

CM to Dm

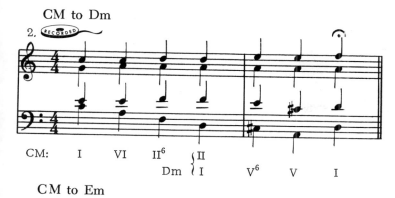

CM: I   VI   II^6 {II
          Dm { I   V^6 V   I

CM to Em

CM: I   VI   V   {III
          Em { I   II^6 I$^6_4$ V   I

CM to GM

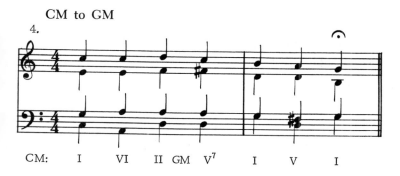

CM: I   VI   II   GM   V^7 I   V   I

CM to Am

CM   I   VI   V^6 I   Am   V $^4_3$ I   V

Cm to E$^\flat$M

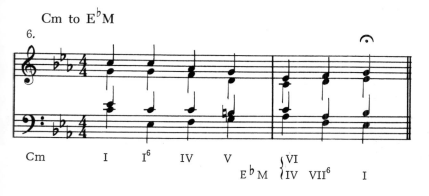

Cm   I   I^6 IV   V   {VI
          E$^\flat$M {IV   VII^6 I

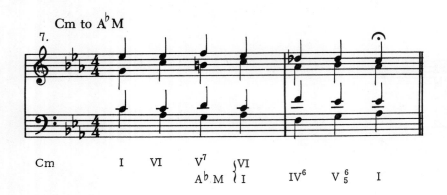

Cm to A♭M

Cm   I   VI   V⁷   {VI
                     A♭M   {I   IV⁶   V⁶₅   I

HARMONY UNIT NO. 15

A. RECOGNITION OF MAJOR, MINOR, AUGMENTED, AND DIMINISHED TRIADS

To the Student: The instructor will play four triads in succession—one major, one minor, one diminished, and one augmented.

Directions: Write the order in which these triads are played. Use:

Major—M   Minor—m   Diminished—D   Augmented—A

To the Teacher: Play each set of triads at a speed of about MM 60. This is an exercise designed to encourage quick perception.

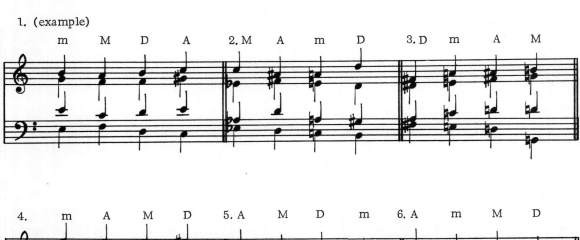

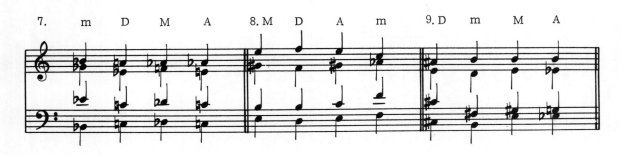

HARMONY UNIT NO. 15

B. DICTATION OF FOUR PART EXERCISES

To the Student: Notes are missing from these four part harmonizations.

Directions:
1. Complete all four parts on the staff.
2. Make a complete harmonic analysis.
3. Exercises No. 5 and 6 contain non-harmonic tones. Add these to the staff and identify the type of each.

To the Teacher: Play at a speed of two seconds per chord. Three or four playings should be sufficient.

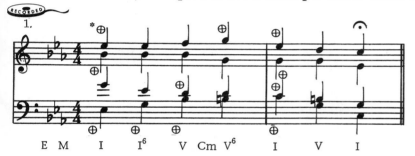

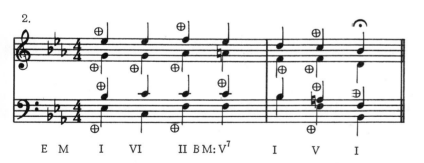

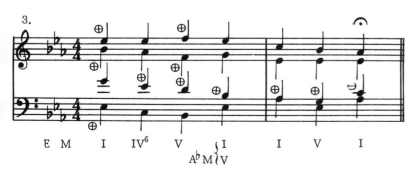

*⊕ indicates note is given in Student Workbook.

187

4.

Cm   I   V⁶   VI   II⁶

♭Bᵇ M { III⁶ / IV⁶   V⁶   I

5.

GM   I   I   V⁶   I

CM { IV⁶ / I⁶   IV   V   I

6.

FM VI   V₆   I   VII⁶   I⁶   II ⁶₅   V   I

HARMONY UNIT NO. 15

Workbook Page 155

C. DICTATION OF EXERCISES IN MODULATION

To the Student: A phrase in four part harmony will be played by the instructor.

Directions:
1. Write the soprano voice on the staff.
2. Write the bass voice on the staff.
3. Make a complete harmonic analysis including modulation.
   Optional for advanced students:
4. Add also the alto and tenor voices on the staff.

To the Teacher:
1. Play the tonic (I) chord in the key, then the first chord of the exercise to give students the starting notes—none are given in the Student Workbook.
2. Play once or twice emphasizing the soprano line.
3. Play once or twice emphasizing the bass line.
4. Play once or twice (slower) for analysis of each chord.

188

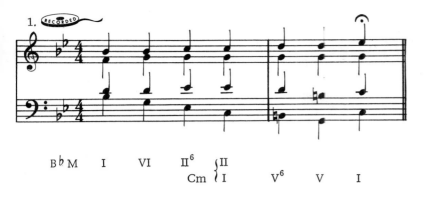

1.

B♭ M   I   VI   II⁶ { II
             Cm { I   V⁶   V   I

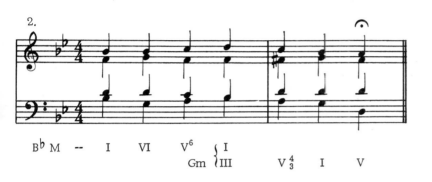

2.

B♭ M -- I   VI   V⁶ { I
             Gm { III   V $\frac{4}{3}$ I   V

3.

Cm -- I   VI   V⁷ { VI
           A♭ M { I   IV⁶   V $\frac{6}{5}$ I

4.

GM   I   V⁵   CM V $\frac{4}{2}$ I⁶   Am V $\frac{4}{2}$ I⁶   V⁶   V   I

5.

DM -- III V⁶ V I Em V⁶ I V⁷ I

6.

FM -- I I⁶ V {I / V} II I⁶ V VI
B♭M

Workbook Page 156

HARMONY UNIT NO. 15

D. DICTATION OF NON-HARMONIC TONES

To the Student: Each exercise consists of a two chord figure containing a non-harmonic tone. The instructor will play each exercise for you.

Directions:
1. Complete all four voices (including non-harmonic tones).
2. Name the type of non-harmonic tone:
   Unaccented passing tone—U P T
   Accented passing tone—A P T (some texts call this an appoggiatura)
   Suspension—S
   Neighboring tone—N T
   Appoggiatura—A
   Escape tone (echappee)—E T
   Anticipation—A N T

To the Teacher: Play two or three times at a speed of one chord per two or three seconds. The first chord in each exercise is given in the Student Workbook.

1. RECORDED 2. 3. 4. 5.

ANT APT NT SUS APP

190

SUS   NT   APT   UPT   ET

ANT   UPT   SUS   APT   UPT

SUS   ET   APT   SUS   NT

HARMONY UNIT NO. 16

Workbook Page 158

A. REVIEW OF ALL TRIADS AND THE V⁷ CHORD

To the Student: Two short harmonic exercises will be played—the second immediately following the first. The basic chord structure (disregarding different inversions of the same chord) may or may not be the same in both exercises. Listen carefully for the basic chord pattern (I, IV, VI, etc.) whatever it may be.

Directions:
1. If the two exercises have the *same* chords (perhaps in different arrangements) mark "same" in the blank.
2. If the two exercises have *different* chords, mark "different" in the blank.

To the Teacher: Play the first set of progressions, pause slightly, then play the second set. Play at an approximate speed of MM 44 to 60 per chord.

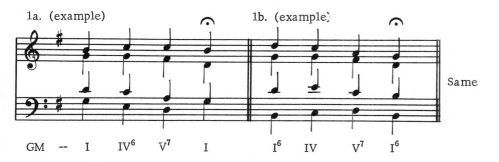

Same

GM --   I   IV⁶   V⁷   I   I⁶   IV   V⁷   I⁶

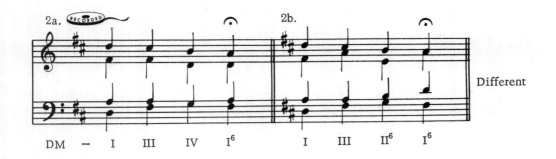

Different

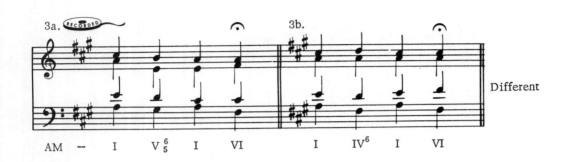

Different

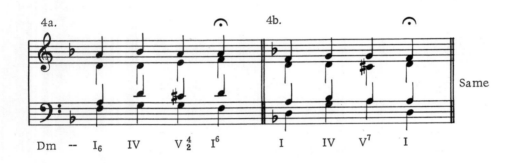

Same

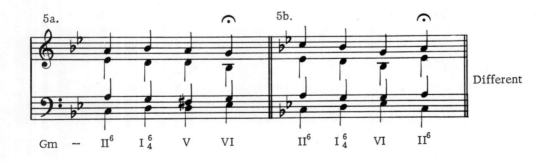

Different

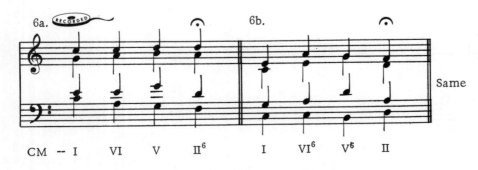

Same

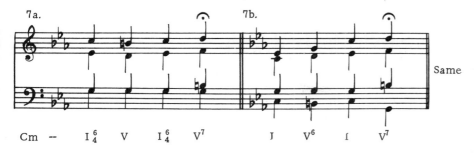

Cm --   I⁶₄   V   I⁶₄   V⁷   I   V⁶   I   V⁷   Same

Workbook Page 158

HARMONY UNIT NO. 16
B. BASS FACTORS, SOPRANO FACTORS, CHORD QUALITY

To the Student: Following is a series of isolated notes. These represent the bass notes of chords. The teacher will play the four-part chords.

Directions:
1. Write the soprano factor in the space above the staff.
2. Write the bass factor in the space beneath the staff.
3. Write the soprano note on the staff in notation.
4. Write the quality (M, m, D, Mm) in the second space below the bass.
Optional:
5. Write *all* the notes of the chord on the staff.

To the Teacher: Play each chord slowly and all tones simultaneously. Emphasize particular voices only if absolutely necessary.

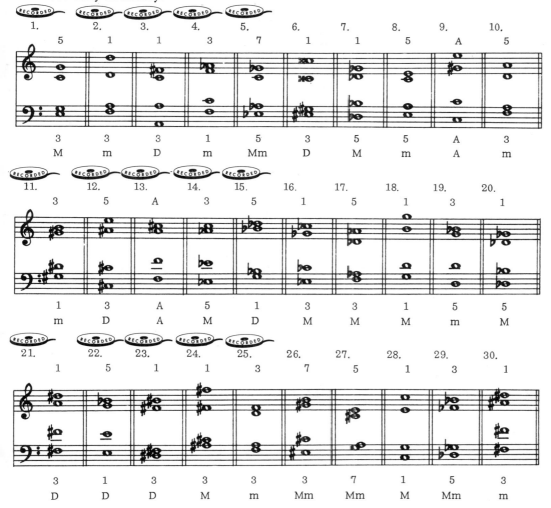

193

HARMONY UNIT NO. 16

C. KEY FEELING

To the Student: In each of the following exercises you will hear a series of four chords. The third chord of each group is written out completely. Each of the series will convey a definite key feeling. In your own mind try to determine the analysis of the third chord, and from that you can determine the key of the exercise.

Directions:

1. Write the key of the exercise in the proper blank.
2. Write the key signature at the beginning (on the staff).
3. Write the soprano melody on the staff.
4. Write the bass melody on the staff.
5. Write the analysis of the given chord (third chord).

Optional for advanced students:

6. Write the alto and tenor notes also on the staff.
7. Write the analysis of all four chords.

To the Teacher: Play the chords at a speed of about 40 to 60 MM. Two playings should be sufficient.

HARMONY UNIT NO. 16
D. RECOGNITION OF CHORD PROGRESSIONS

To the Student: In these exercises you will be given only the final soprano and bass note of a four chord series.

Directions:
1. Write the soprano melody on the staff.
2. Write the bass melody on the staff.
3. Write the key signature at the beginning.
4. Write a Roman Numeral analysis of the chords.
Optional for advanced students:
5. Write also the alto and tenor voice on the staff.

To the Teacher: Play each exercise at an approximate speed of MM 40 to 60 per chord. Two or three playings should be sufficient.
Final bass and soprano note is given in Student Workbook.

A♭M   I   IV   I⁶₄   V

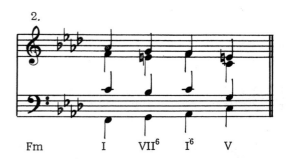

Fm   I   VII⁶   I⁶   V

F♯m   I⁶   I   V⁷   I

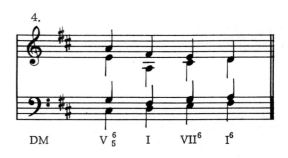

DM   V⁶₅   I   VII⁶   I⁶

Bm --   V⁷   V⁷   I⁶₄   V⁷

FM --   I   I   IV⁶   V⁶

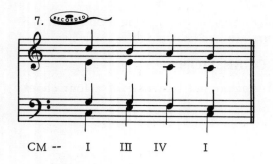

CM --   I   III   IV   I

E♭M --   I   V $\frac{6}{5}$ I   V⁷

Gm --   I   V⁷   VI   V

INTRODUCTION
RHYTHM UNITS

It is wise in presenting the Rhythm Units to connect and unify the methods as much as possible with those methods used in rhythmic sight reading. Instructional methods in rhythmic sight reading differ from instructor to instructor, but generally fall into one of the following discipline types:

1. Instructor introduces a system of rhythmic syllables which correspond to note values. Students then proceed with rhythmic sight singing, reducing the melody to a single neutral pitch, and singing the rhythmic syllables to correspond with the durational values. Rhythmic syllables in widespread usage today consist of two main types (with occasional modifications depending upon the instructor):

Students see the following composition:

Students respond by singing:

Type I: 1   and 3 a andu 4   and 2   4 a and
Type II: 1   te 3 ta te ta 4   te 2   4 ta te

2. Instructor introduces various conductors' beats. Students learn to beat time and sing along with the arm and hand motions. Some instructors insist that the students use both the rhythmic syllables (described above) *and* the conductor's beat in rhythmic sight singing.

3. Some instructors insist that rhythmic syllables inhibit the students and are actually a drawback to smooth and uninterrupted rhythmic sight reading. These instructors have students sing the melodies on a neutral pitch *and* a neutral syllable (such as "la" or "ta").

4. Some instructors prefer to have students clap the rhythms. This system has its merits, but durational values of long notes are difficult to accommodate in this procedure.

5. In certain situations where it is expedient the instructor has the students play rhythmic exercises on the piano either on neutral pitch or duplicating the melody as it is written (with varying pitch).

Infinite variations, permutations, and combinations are possible with the basic five types listed above. Scarcely any two instructors use exactly the same approach. No matter what method of rhythmic sight reading is presented the Rhythm Units in this book will not conflict. To the contrary the Rhythm Units are intended as ear training aids to any accepted discipline and if properly administered will act as a valuable adjunct to a complete rhythmic training in the first year of music theory.

A few days after the basic drills in rhythmic sight reading have been initiated the Rhythm Units may be taken up. As with the Melody Units the instructor can give much material aid to students by instituting some primary drills in class which will be helpful in effecting smooth and accurate rhythmic dictation. Some standard procedures which have proven effective in the past are:

1. Do not permit students to write rhythmic dictation on paper until they can repeat back the phrase or section as it was dictated. If the instructor uses rhythmic syllables the students should learn to sing back the dictated phrase to him in rhythmic syllables. If he employs the method of clapping rhythms, the students should clap back the dictated sections.

2. Most students will experience no difficulty in notating rhythm once they have memorized the dictated passage. A few students have difficulty making the transition from sound patterns they hear to notational patterns they see. Students of this type usually constitute only a small minority of a class, but deserve special treatment. Visual symbols that are more simple than regular notation are frequently employed for these few students. An illustration is given here:

SIMPLE TIME		COMPOUND TIME	
one beat value	- -	one beat value	- -
half beat value	- -	one third beat value	- -
quarter beat value	- -	one-sixth beat value	- -
eighth beat value	- -	one-twelfth beat value	- -

Thus, the following measure:

would be interpreted as:

or, the following measure:

would be interpreted as:

It must be remembered that this system is suggested only as a last resort, and the average or above average student will not need such synthetic methods to effect smooth and accurate rhythmic dictation. Even in the case of the desperate few the "vertical line" system should be used for only a short time lest the students come to rely on the "crutch" as a necessity.

3. As a class drill for any of the exercises in the Rhythm Units the instructor divides the class into two equal groups. One group recites the beats of the dictated exercise while the other half recites the rhythmic syllables (or claps the rhythms). An illustration is given:

Instructor plays:

One half the class recites:

one   two   three   one   two   three

while the other half the class recites:

one du 2   one a an du 2   and   3
or: one ta 2   one ta te ta 2   te   3

The above suggested class drills to prepare students for the Rhythm Units are but a few of the many possible. It must be remembered that rhythm must be felt and experienced as a sensation before it can be truly understood. Those methods which take advantage of this fact are most likely to be successful. Almost any method which takes advantage of physical response to rhythm is advantageous. Clapping certainly accomplishes this goal as does the employment of a "conductors' beat" with recitation of rhythmic syllables.

As in the Melody Units and Harmony Units the Rhythm Units present various aspects of rhythmic dictation. Three main types are used:

1. Type I—Requires the students to write music notation. This exercise type is the backbone of rhythmic dictation. It is usually considered the most difficult to solve, and is certainly of great beneficial value. Example: Rhythm Unit No. 1, Section B.

2. Type II—Requires students to pass judgment on notation already written for the students. Two sub-types are represented in this book.

Sub-type a—Notation written out which does not agree with dictated sound. Example: Rhythm Unit No. 11, Section A.

Sub-type b—Multiple choice in which students are given several possible correct versions from which to choose. Example: Rhythm Unit No. 1, Section A.

3. Type III—Requires students to arrange or clarify correct notation partially completed. Example: Rhythm Unit No. 2, Section A.

The Rhythm Units found in this book are intended to be used in conjunction with any of the known procedures. The Rhythm Units were designed especially with the idea in mind that they could lend themselves to any "method" preferred by any individual instructor. To this end it is anticipated that instructors will seek to adapt them to his own needs, and not permit them to adapt him.

Workbook Page 163

RHYTHM UNIT NO. 1

A. SIMPLE METER. ONE AND TWO BEAT VALUES. MULTIPLE CHOICE

To the Student: Each exercise consists of a rhythm (played four times in succession by the teacher) chosen from the group of four (a. b. c. d.) possibilities which you see. Listen carefully as the teacher plays the rhythm and repeats it.

Directions: Circle the letter (a. b. c. d.) which represents the correct rhythm played.

To the Teacher: If students have difficulty with this set of exercises, have them clap the rhythm and say the meter immediately after you play it. Experiencing the rhythm themselves usually clarifies their thinking and makes the correct answer obvious. Usually one playing is sufficient, but do not hesitate to play the exercises again if needed by the students. Dictation is a new procedure for most students.

RHYTHM UNIT NO. 1

B. INCOMPLETED EXERCISES IN SIMPLE METER. ONE AND TWO BEAT VALUES

To the Student: The teacher will play a short rhythmic exercise. The first measure of each exercise is completed for you.

Directions: Complete the rhythm of the exercise on a neutral pitch.

To the Teacher: You may wish to have the student memorize each exercise before writing it down. Have the students say the meter and clap the rhythm.

⊕ indicates notes given in Student Workbook.

RHYTHM UNIT NO. 1

Workbook Page 165

C. METER SIGNATURES

To the Student: Each exercise consists of a complete composition of several measures. Listen carefully to determine the meter.

Directions: Write the correct meter signature in the blank provided. Use only: 2 3 4
4 4 4

To the Teacher: Play each exercise at a steady and comfortable tempo. At this stage of the student's development it might be wise to emphasize the metric beats slightly. Metronome markings and details of interpretation have been purposely omitted from the score in order to give wider latitude for the instructor to employ his own preferences.

Workbook Page 166

A. TWO BEAT VALUE SYNCOPATIONS. SIMPLE METER

To the Student: These exercises are correctly written except that they lack bar lines and meter signatures.

Directions:
1. Write the meter signature on the staff in the proper place.
2. Add bar lines in the correct places.

These exercises will employ meter signature selected from the following:

2	3	4		2	3	4		2	3	4		2	3	4
2	2	2		4	4	4		8	8	8		16	16	16

To the Teacher:
1. Tap or say the unit metrical beat before beginning the composition. Use an odd number of beats (perhaps 5) to avoid giving away the correct meter signature at this time.
2. Play once or twice at a tempo of MM 100. If students are confused, emphasize the first beat of each measure slightly.

1.

2.

3.

4.

5.

6.

RHYTHM UNIT NO. 2
B. INCOMPLETED EXERCISES IN SIMPLE METER. HALF-BEAT VALUES INTRODUCED

To the Student: Each exercise consists of a short rhythmic phrase. The first note value of each exercise is given.

Directions: Complete each exercise on the staff in notation. Use a neutral pitch.

To the Teacher: When students have difficulty tap the meter with the left hand and play the rhythm with the right hand. Experiment at times playing the rhythm on a neutral pitch rather than using the melody given.

⊕ indicates notes given in Student Workbook.

RHYTHM UNIT NO. 2

Workbook Page 168

C. METER SIGNATURES

To the Student: Each exercise consists of a complete composition of several measures. Listen carefully to determine the meter.

> **Directions:** Write the correct meter signature in the blank provided. Use only: $\frac{2}{4}$ $\frac{3}{4}$ $\frac{4}{4}$

To the Teacher: Play each exercise at a steady and comfortable tempo. At this stage of the student's development it might be wise to emphasize the metric beats slightly.

RHYTHM UNIT NO. 3

Workbook Page 169

A. DETECTION OF ERRORS

To the Student: Each exercise consists of six or eight measures of music. Each measure is numbered. In each exercise THERE ARE ERRORS IN TWO MEASURES (place where the notation does not correspond with what is played).

Directions: Circle the numbers of the measures in which the notation is different from that played by the teacher. Each exercise has two measures which do not match the version as played by the teacher.

To the Teacher: Play each exercise at about MM 100-150 per beat unit. Increase the speed even further if the students have no difficulty.

RHYTHM UNIT NO. 3

B. INCOMPLETED EXERCISES. HALF-BEAT VALUES INTRODUCED

To the Student: Each exercise consists of a short phrase of music. The first note value of each exercise is given.

   Directions: Complete each exercise on the staff in notation. Use a neutral pitch.

To the Teacher: When students have difficulty tap the meter with the left hand and play the rhythm with the right hand. Experiment at times playing the rhythm on a neutral pitch rather than using the melody given.

   ⊕ indicates notes given in Student Workbook.

RHYTHM UNIT NO. 3

C. SIMPLE METER

Workbook Page 171

To the Student: These exercises are correctly written except that they lack bar lines and meter signatures.

Directions:
1. Write the meter signature on the staff in the proper place.
2. Add bar lines in the correct places.

These exercises will employ meter signatures selected from the following:

2	3	4	2	3	4	2	3	4	2	3	4
2	2	2	4	4	4	8	8	8	16	16	16

To the Teacher:
1. Tap or say the unit metrical beat before beginning the composition. Use an odd number of beats (perhaps 5) to avoid giving away the correct meter signature at this time.
2. Play once or twice at a tempo of MM 100. If students are confused, emphasize the first beat of each measure slightly.

RHYTHM UNIT NO. 4

A. SIMPLE METER, HALF-BEAT VALUES EMPHASIZED

To the Student: The teacher will play a short rhythmic exercise. The first measure of each exercise is completed for you.

Directions: Complete the rhythm of the exercise on the staff (use a neutral pitch).

To the Teacher:
1. Play the exercise once or twice.
2. Have students clap or say the exercise as you played it.
3. When students clap or say the exercise accurately, they should then write it on paper.
THE FIRST MEASURE OF EACH EXERCISE IS GIVEN IN THE STUDENT WORKBOOK.

RHYTHM UNIT NO. 4

B. MULTIPLE CHOICE. HALF-BEAT VALUES EMPHASIZED

To the Student: Each exercise consists of a rhythm (played four times in succession by the teacher) chosen from the group of four (a. b. c. d.) possibilities which you see. Listen carefully as the teacher plays the rhythm and repeats it.

Directions: Circle the letter (a. b. c. d.) which represents the correct rhythm played.

To the Teacher: If students have difficulty with this set of exercises, have them clap the rhythm and say the meter immediately after you play it. Experiencing the rhythm themselves usually clarifies their thinking and makes the correct answer obvious.

13. (a)

14. (b)

Workbook Page 175

RHYTHM UNIT NO. 4

C. SIMPLE METER. TWO VOICE EXERCISES

To the Student: Each exercise is a two voice rhythmc phrase. The instructor will play the exercise in its completed form.

 Directions: Add the missing rhythmic values to the staff (on a neutral pitch).

To the Teacher: Play each of the following exercises at a steady and comfortable tempo.

 THE FIRST MEASURE OF EACH EXERCISE IS GIVEN IN BOTH VOICES IN THE STUDENT WORKBOOK.

1. RECORDED

2.

3.

RHYTHM UNIT NO. 5

A. MULTIPLE CHOICE. HALF-BEAT VALUES EMPHASIZED

To the Student: Each exercise consists of a rhythm (played four times in succession by the teacher) chosen from the group of four (a. b. c. d.) possibilities which you see. Listen carefully as the teacher plays the rhythm and repeats it.

Directions: Circle the letter (a. b. c. d.) which represents the correct rhythm played.

To the Teacher: If students have difficulty with this set of exercises, have them clap the rhythm and say the meter immediately after you play it. Experiencing the rhythm themselves usually clarifies their thinking and makes the correct answer obvious.

13. (c)

14. (a)

Workbook Page 179

RHYTHM UNIT NO. 5

B. SIMPLE METER. HALF-BEAT VALUES IN SYNCOPATION

To the Student: The teacher will play a short rhythmic exercise. The first measure of each exercise is completed for you.

Directions: Complete the rhythm on the staff (use a neutral pitch).

To the Teacher:
1. Play the exercise once or twice.
2. Have students clap or say the exercise as you played it.
3. When students clap or say the exercise accurately, they should then write it on paper.

THE FIRST MEASURE OF EACH EXERCISE IS GIVEN IN THE STUDENT WORKBOOK.

RHYTHM UNIT NO. 5
C. SIMPLE METER. HALF-BEAT VALUES IN SYNCOPATION

To the Student: These exercises are correctly written except that they lack bar lines and meter signatures.

Directions:
1. Write the meter signature on the staff in the proper place.
2. Add bar lines in the correct places.

These exercises will employ meter signatures selected from the following:

2	3	4	2	3	4	2	3	4	2	3	4
2	2	2	4	4	4	8	8	8	16	16	16

To the Teacher:
1. Tap or say the unit metrical beat before beginning the composition. Use an odd number of beats (perhaps 5) to avoid giving away the correct meter signature at this time.
2. Play once or twice at a tempo of MM 100. If students are confused, emphasize the first beat of each measure slightly.

6.

RHYTHM UNIT NO. 6

A. SIMPLE METER. INTRODUCTION OF QUARTER BEAT VALUES

To the Student: Each exercise consists of a rhythm (played twice in succession by the teacher) chosen from the group of three (a. b. c.) possibilities which you see. Listen carefully as the teacher plays the rhythm and repeats it.

Directions: Circle the letter (a. b. c.) which represents the correct rhythm played.

To the Teacher:
1. Tap one measure before beginning the exercise.
2. Play the exercise.
3. Have students immediately tap or say the exercise back exactly as you played it.
4. When students have accurately memorized the exercise, they are ready to indicate their choice on paper.

1. (b)

2. (a)

3. (b)

4. (c)

5. (c)

6. (a)

RHYTHM UNIT NO. 6
B. SIMPLE METER. QUARTER BEAT VALUES

To the Student: The teacher will play a short rhythmic exercise. The first measure of each exercise is completed for you.

Directions: Complete the rhythm of the exercise on a neutral pitch.

To the Teacher:
1. Play the exercise once or twice.
2. Have students immediately tap or say the exercise back exactly as you played it.
3. When students have accurately memorized the exercise, they are ready to write their answer on paper.

THE FIRST MEASURE OF EACH EXERCISE IS GIVEN IN THE STUDENT WORKBOOK.

1.

2.

3.

4.

5.

6.

7. Haydn--Trio No. 1 in G, 3rd Movement

8. Tschaikovsky--Symphony No. 6, 3rd Movement

RHYTHM UNIT NO. 6

C. SIMPLE METER. QUARTER BEAT VALUES

To the Student: These exercises are correctly written except that they lack bar lines and meter signatures.

Directions:
1. Write the meter signature on the staff in the proper place.
2. Add bar lines in the correct places.

These exercises will employ meter signatures selected from the following:

2	3	4	2	3	4	2	3	4	2	3	4
2	2	2	4	4	4	8	8	8	16	16	16

To the Teacher:
1. Tap or say the unit metrical beat before beginning the composition. Use an odd number of beats (perhaps 5) to avoid giving away the correct meter signature at this time.
2. Play once or twice at a tempo of MM 100. If students are confused, emphasize the first beat of each measure slightly.

1.

2.

3.

4. Tschaikovsky--Piano Trio, Op. 50

5. Weber--Invitation to the Dance, Op. 65

6. Wagner--Die Meistersinger

7. Concerto in G, K216 (For Violin and Orchestra)

8.

Workbook Page 185

RHYTHM UNIT NO. 7

A. SIMPLE METER. INTRODUCTION OF THE BEAT UNIT DIVIDED INTO TRIPLETS

To the Student: Each exercise consists of a rhythm (played twice in succession by the teacher) chosen from the group of three (a. b. c.) possibilities which you see. Listen carefully as the teacher plays the rhythm and repeats it.

Directions: Circle the letter (a. b. c.) which represents the correct rhythm played.

To the Teacher:
1. Tap one measure before beginning the exercise.
2. Play the exercise.
3. Have students immediately tap or say the exercise back exactly as you played it.
4. When students have accurately memorized the exercise, they are ready to indicate their choice on paper.

1. (c)

2. (b)

RHYTHM UNIT NO. 7

B. SIMPLE METER. BEAT UNIT DIVIDED INTO TRIPLETS

To the Student: The teacher will play a short rhythmic exercise. The first measure of each exercise is completed for you.

Directions: Complete the rhythm on the staff (use a neutral pitch).

To the Teacher:
1. Play the exercise twice.
2. Have the students immediately tap or say the exercise back exactly as you played it.
3. When students have accurately memorized the exercise, they are ready to write their answers on paper.

THE FIRST MEASURE OF EACH EXERCISE IS GIVEN IN THE STUDENT WORKBOOK.

Workbook Page 188

RHYTHM UNIT NO. 7

C. SIMPLE METER. BEAT UNIT DIVIDED INTO TRIPLETS

To the Student: These exercises are correctly written except that they lack bar lines and meter signatures.

Directions:

1. Write the meter signature on the staff in the proper place.
2. Add bar lines in the correct places.

These exercises will employ meter signatures selected from the following:

```
2   3   4     2   3   4     2   3   4     2   3   4
2   2   2     4   4   4     8   8   8     16 16 16
```

To the Teacher:

1. Tap or say the unit metrical beat before beginning the composition. Use an odd number of beats (perhaps 5) to avoid giving away the correct meter signature at this time.
2. Play once or twice at a tempo of MM 100. If students are confused, emphasize the first beat of each measure slightly.

1. Beethoven -- German Dance

2.

3.

4.

5.

6.

7. Mozart--Quartet, K 499, 4th Movement

8. Brahms--Concerto for Violin and Orchestra, Op. 77

Workbook Page 189

RHYTHM UNIT NO. 8

A. COMPOUND METER. INTRODUCTION OF COMPOUND METER

To the Student: The teacher will play a short rhythmic exercise. The first measure of each exercise is completed for you.

Directions: Complete the rhythm of the exercise on a neutral pitch.

To the Teacher:
1. Play the exercise once or twice.
2. Have students immediately tap or say the exercise back exactly as you played it.
3. When students have accurately memorized the exercise, they are ready to write their answer on paper.

THE FIRST MEASURE OF EACH EXERCISE IS GIVEN IN THE STUDENT WORKBOOK.

RHYTHM UNIT NO. 8

Workbook Page 190

B. MULTIPLE CHOICE. COMPOUND METER

To the Student: Each exercise consists of a rhythm (played twice in succession by the teacher) chosen from the group of three (a. b. c.) possibilities which you see. Listen carefully as the teacher plays the rhythm and repeats it.

Directions: Circle the letter (a. b. c.) which represents the correct rhythm played.

To the Teacher: If students have difficulty with this set of exercises, have them clap the rhythm and say the meter immediately after you play it. Experiencing the rhythm themselves usually clarifies their thinking and makes the correct answer obvious.

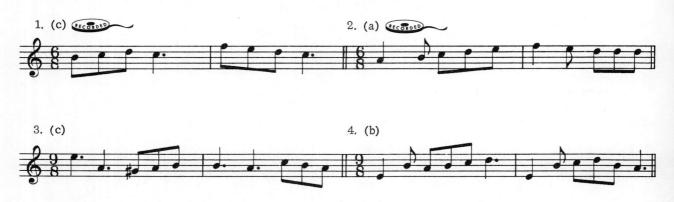

RHYTHM UNIT NO. 8

C. COMPOUND METER

To the Student: These exercises are correctly written except that they lack bar lines and meter signatures.

Directions:
1. Write the meter signature on the staff in the proper places.
2. Add bar lines in the correct places.

These exercises will employ meter signatures selected from the following:

2	3	4		2	3	4		2	3	4
2	2	2		4	4	4		8	8	8

	6	9	12		6	9	12		6	9	12
	4	4	4		8	8	8		16	16	16

227

To the Teacher:

1. Tap or say the unit metrical beat before beginning the composition. Use an odd number of beats (perhaps 5) to avoid giving away the correct meter signature at this time.
2. Play once or twice at a tempo of MM 100. If the students are confused, emphasize the first beat of each measure slightly.

1. Mozart--German Dances, K 509

2. Mozart--Piano Concerto, K 595

3. Brahms--Piano Quartet, Op. 25

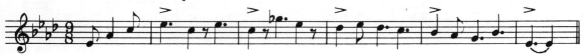

4. Brahms--Violin and Piano Sonata, Op. 78

5. Brahms--Symphony No. 4, Op. 98, 3rd Movement

6. Beethoven--Symphony No. 7, Op. 92, 1st Movement

7. Bach--French Suite No. 5, Gigue

8. Bach--English Suite No. 6, Sarabande

228

RHYTHM UNIT NO. 9

A. INTRODUCTION OF COMPOUND METERS WITH HALF SUB-BEAT VALUES

To the Student: Each exercise consists of a rhythm (played twice in succession by the teacher) chosen from the group of three (a. b. c.) possibilities which you see. Listen carefully as the teacher plays the rhythm and repeats it.

Directions: Circle the letter (a. b. c.) which represents the correct rhythm played.

To the Teacher:

1. Tap one measure before beginning the exercise.
2. Play the exercise.
3. Have students immediately tap or say the exercise back exactly as you played it.
4. When students have accurately memorized the exercise, they are ready to indicate their choice on paper.

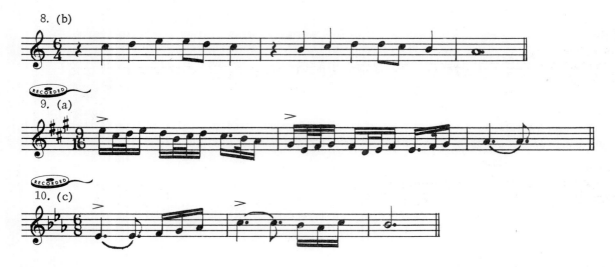

Workbook Page 195

RHYTHM UNIT NO. 9
B. COMPOUND METERS WITH HALF SUB-BEAT VALUES

To the Student: The teacher will play a short rhythmic exercise. Part or all of the first measure of each exercise is completed for you.

   Directions: Complete the rhythm of the exercise on a neutral pitch.

To the Teacher:
1. Play the exercise once or twice.
2. Have students immediately tap or say the exercise exactly as you played it.
3. When students have accurately memorized the exercise, they are ready to complete the exercise on paper.

*"⊕" indicates note is given in Student Workbook.

13. Mendelssohn -- Rondo Capriccioso, Op. 14

14. Mendelssohn -- Songs Without Words, Op. 53, No. 4

15. Mendelssohn -- Songs Without Words, Op. 38, No. 5

16.

17.

18.

*"⊕" indicates the note is given in the Student Workbook.

19.

20.

RHYTHM UNIT NO. 9

C. COMPOUND METERS WITH HALF SUB-BEAT VALUES

To the Student: These exercises are correctly written except that they lack bar lines and meter signatures.

Directions:

1. Write the meter signatures on the staff in the proper place.
2. Add bar lines in the correct places.

These exercises will employ meter signatures selected from the following:

2	3	4	2	3	4	6	9	12	6	9	12
2	2	2	4	4	4	4	4	4	8	8	8

To the Teacher:

1. Tap or say the unit metrical beat before beginning the composition. Use an odd number of beats (perhaps 5) to avoid giving away the correct meter signature at this time.
2. Play once or twice at a tempo of MM 100. If students are confused, emphasize the first beat of each measure slightly.

1.

2. Mendelssohn--Songs Without Words, Op. 67, No. 4

3. Lully--Alceste

4. Liszt--Hungarian Rhapsody, No. 12

5. Haydn--Symphony in A, 4th Movement

6. Gluck--Iphigenia in Aulis, Overture

7. Glinka--Russian and Ludmilla, Overture

8. Bach--Jesus, Joy of Man's Desiring

Workbook Page 199   # RHYTHM UNIT NO. 10

A. INTRODUCTION OF THE SUBDIVIDED TRIPLET IN SIMPLE METER

To the Student: Each exercise consists of a rhythm (played twice in succession by the teacher) chosen from the group of three (a. b. c.) possibilities which you see. Listen carefully as the teacher plays the rhythm and repeats it.

Directions: Circle the letter (a. b. c.) which represents the correct rhythm played.

To the Teacher:
1. Tap one measure before beginning the exercise.
2. Play the exercise.
3. Have students immediately tap or say the exercise back exactly as you played it.
4. When students have accurately memorized the exercise, they are ready to indicate their choice on paper.

1. (c) RECORDED

2. (c) RECORDED

234

RHYTHM UNIT NO. 10

Workbook Page 201

B. SUBDIVIDED TRIPLET IN SIMPLE METER

To the Student: The teacher will play a short rhythmic exercise. The first measure of each exercise is completed for you.

Directions: Complete the rhythm of the exercise on a neutral pitch.

To the Teacher:
1. Play the exercise once or twice.
2. Have students immediately tap or say the exercise back exactly as you played it.
3. When students have accurately memorized the exercise, they are ready to write it on paper.

THE FIRST MEASURE OF EACH EXERCISE IS GIVEN IN THE STUDENT WORKBOOK.

RHYTHM UNIT NO. 10
C. MORE DIFFICULT RHYTHMS IN TWO VOICE EXERCISES

To the Student: Below is a series of incompleted two voice rhythmic exercises. You will hear the exercises in their completed form.

Directions: Add the missing rhythmic values to both voices.

To the Teacher: Try to avoid undue stress on either voice in dictating these exercises.

*Bracket indicates note or notes indicates note is given in Student Workbook.

237

RHYTHM UNIT NO. 11
A. INTRODUCTION OF THE QUARTOLET IN COMPOUND METER

To the Student: The teacher will play the exercises below, but on ONE beat (indicated by numbers 1 - 2 - 3 etc.) he will not play the rhythm which is written.

Directions: Circle the number indicating the beat which is not played as written. In each exercise only ONE number will be circled.

To the Teacher: Although these exercises are notated to be played in a melodic fashion they may be rapped, tapped, or played on a neutral pitch if the instructor so desires.

*The circle indicates the beat which is incorrectly notated in the Student Workbook.

RHYTHM UNIT NO. 11

Workbook Page 205

B. QUARTOLET IN COMPOUND METER

To the Student: The teacher will play a short rhythmic exercise. The first measure of each exercise is completed for you.

Directions: Complete the rhythm on a neutral pitch.

To the Teacher:

1. Play the exercise once or twice.
2. Have the students immediately tap or say the exercise back exactly as you played it. If the exercise is too long, divide it into sections.
3. When the students have accurately memorized the exercise, they are ready to write it down.

THE FIRST MEASURE OF EACH EXERCISE IS GIVEN IN THE STUDENT WORKBOOK.

RHYTHM UNIT NO. 11

Workbook Page 206

C. QUARTOLET IN COMPOUND METER

To the Student: These exercises are correctly written except that they lack bar lines and meter signatures.

Directions:
1. Write the meter signature on the staff in the proper place.
2. Add bar lines in the correct places.

These exercises will employ meter signatures selected from the following:

2 3 4   2 3 4   6 9 12
2 2 2   4 4 4   8 8 8

To the Teacher:
1. Tap or say the unit metrical beat before beginning the composition. Use an odd number of beats (perhaps 5) to avoid giving away the correct meter signature at this time.
2. Play once or twice at a tempo of MM 100. If students are confused, emphasize the first beat of each measure slightly.

240

RHYTHM UNIT NO. 12

A. SIMPLE AND COMPOUND METER. INTRODUCTION OF THE BASIC BEAT DIVIDED IN EIGHTHS IN SIMPLE METER

To the Student: Below is a series of incompleted rhythmic exercises. You will hear the exercises in their completed form.

Directions: Write the missing rhythmic values on the staff in music notation. Do not try to indicate the pitch of the notes—only the rhythm.

To the Teacher: Play each of the following excerpts at a steady and comfortable tempo. Although these are written in pitch notation they may be dictated by tapping on the piano or playing a neutral pitch if the instructor so desires.

---

*Bracket indicates note or notes given in the Student Workbook.

3. Mozart--Fantasy in D Minor, K 397

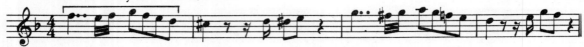

4. Mozart--Rondo in D, K 485

RECORDED

5. Tschaikovsky--1812 Festival Overture, Op. 49

6. Wagner--Tristan Und Isolde

7. Wagner--Gotterdammerung

8. Mascagni--Cavalleria Rusticana

9. Schubert--Opus 51, No. 2 for Piano

10. Schrecker--Kleine Suite

242

11. Rimsky-Korsakov--Le Coq D'Or, Suite

12. Mussorgsky--A Night on Bald Mountain

Workbook Page 209

RHYTHM UNIT NO. 12

B. SIMPLE AND COMPOUND METER. BEAT UNIT SUBDIVIDED IN EIGHTHS

To the Student: Below is a series of three measure rhythmic exercises. In each exercise the notation will agree with the dictated version except on ONE beat only.

Directions: Circle the number indicating the beat which is *not* played as notated.

To the Teacher: Since the problem involved in this set of exercises is a matter of selection rather than dictation, the speed of these exercises may be increased considerably.

―――――――――

*Indicates the beat which disagrees with the version in the Student Workbook.

243

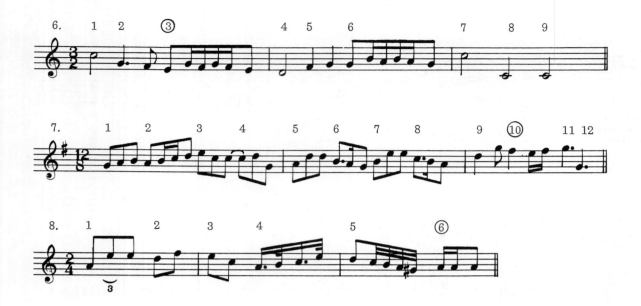

RHYTHM UNIT NO. 12
C. MORE DIFFICULT RHYTHMS IN TWO-VOICE EXERCISES

To the Student: Below is a series of incompleted two-voice rhythmic exercises. You will hear the exercises in their completed form.

Directions: Add the missing rhythmic values to both voices.

To the Teacher: Play each of the following exercises in a completely balanced manner—no unusual dynamic stress in either voice.

*Bracket indicates note or notes given in the Student Workbook.

Workbook Page 212

RHYTHM UNIT NO. 13

A. SIMPLE AND COMPOUND METER. INTRODUCTION OF THE SUPERTRIPLET

To the Student: The teacher will play a short rhythmic exercise. At least one beat (and sometimes as much as a measure) is completed for you.

   Directions: Complete the rhythm on the staff (use a neutral pitch). A SUPERTRIPLET is a triplet which extends over two or more beats in simple time.

To the Teacher:
1. Play the exercise once or twice.
2. Have the students immediately tap or say the exercise back exactly as you played it. In the case of longer exercises divide them into smaller units.
3. When students have accurately memorized the exercise, they are ready to complete the exercise on paper.

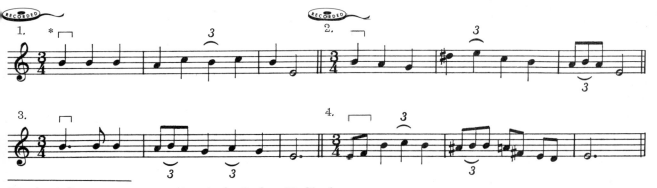

*Bracket indicates note or notes given in the Student Workbook.

17. Beethoven--Serenade, Op. 8 for Violin, Viola, and Cello

18. Beethoven--Serenade, Op. 8 for Violin, Viola, and Cello

Workbook Page 213

RHYTHM UNIT NO. 13

B. SIMPLE AND COMPOUND METER. SUPERTRIPLET

To the Student: Below is a series of short rhythmic exercises. In each exercise the notation will agree with the dictated version except on ONE beat only.

Directions: Circle the number indicating the beat which is *not* played as notated.

To the Teacher: Since the problem involved in this set of exercises is a matter of selection rather than dictation, the speed of these exercises may be increased considerably.

_____

*Circle indicates the beat which disagrees with the Student Workbook.

247

RHYTHM UNIT NO. 13

Workbook Page 215

C. MORE DIFFICULT EXERCISES

To the Student: In these exercises no beginning notes are given to help you. The instructor will count one measure before beginning each exercise.

Directions: Write the rhythm on the staff in notation (use a neutral pitch).

To the Teacher:
1. Count one measure before beginning. The Student Workbook has no beginning note or notes given.
2. Have the student sing the exercises back to you as they were played.
3. When the student can sing the exercise accurately he is ready to complete the exercise on paper.

1. Count:

2. Count:

3. Count:

4. Count:

5. Count:

6. Count:

7. Count:

8. Count:

Workbook Page 216

RHYTHM UNIT NO. 14

A. SIMPLE AND COMPOUND METER. INTRODUCTION OF THE SUBTRIPLET IN BOTH SIMPLE AND COMPOUND METERS

To the Student: The teacher will play a short rhythmic exercise. The first measure of each exercise is completed for you.

Directions: Complete the rhythm of the exercise on a neutral pitch.

To the Teacher:
1. Play the exercise once or twice.
2. Have students immediately tap or say the exercise back exactly as you played it. If some exercises are too long for comprehension, break them into smaller units.
3. When students have accurately memorized the exercise, then they are ready to write their answer on paper.

THE FIRST MEASURE OF EACH EXERCISE IS GIVEN IN THE STUDENT WORKBOOK.

RHYTHM UNIT NO. 14

B. SIMPLE AND COMPOUND METER. SUBTRIPLET IN BOTH SIMPLE AND COMPOUND METERS

To the Student: Below is a series of short rhythmic exercises. In each exercise the notation will agree with the dictated version except on ONE beat only.

Directions: Circle the number indicating the beat which is *not* played as notated.

To the Teacher: Since the problem involved in this set of exercises is a matter of selection rather than dictation, the speed of these exercises may be increased considerably.

*Circle indicates the beat which disagrees with the Student Workbook.

RHYTHM UNIT NO. 14

Workbook Page 218

C. MORE DIFFICULT EXERCISES

To the Student: In these exercises no beginning notes are given to help you. The instructor will count one measure before beginning each exercise.

Directions: Write the rhythm on the staff in notation (use a neutral pitch).

To the Teacher:
1. Count one measure before beginning. The Student Workbook has no beginning note or notes given.
2. Have the student sing the exercises back to you as they were played.
3. When the student can sing the exercise accurately he is ready to complete the exercise on paper.

Workbook Page 220 **RHYTHM UNIT NO. 15**

A. SIMPLE AND COMPOUND METER. INTRODUCTION OF SUBTRIPLETS ON THE QUARTER BEAT IN SIMPLE METER. SUB-BEAT DIVIDED INTO QUARTOLETS IN COMPOUND METER

To the Student: The teacher will play a short rhythmic exercise. The first measure is completed for you.

Directions: Complete the rhythm on the staff.

To the Teacher:

1. Play the exercise once or twice.
2. Have the students immediately tap or say the rhythm back exactly as you played it. In case of longer exercises divide them into smaller units.
3. When students have accurately memorized the rhythm, they are ready to complete the exercise on paper.

THE FIRST MEASURE OF EACH EXERCISE IS GIVEN IN THE STUDENT WORKBOOK.

7. Mozart--Symphony No. 41 (Jupiter), K 551

8. Mozart--Symphony No. 39, K 543

RHYTHM UNIT NO. 15
B. REVIEW OF ALL RHYTHMIC PROBLEMS STUDIED SO FAR

To the Student: Below is a series of short rhythmic exercises. In each exercise the notation will agree with the dictated version except on ONE beat only.

Directions: Circle the number indicating the beat which is *not* played as notated.

To the Teacher: Since the problem involved in this set of exercises is a matter of selection rather than dictation, the speed of these exercises may be increased considerably.

*Circle indicates the beat in the Student Workbook which disagrees with the dictated version.

RHYTHM UNIT NO. 15

C. MORE DIFFICULT EXERCISES

To the Student: In these exercises no beginning notes are given to help you. The instructor will count one measure before beginning each exercise.

Directions: Write the rhythm on the staff in notation (use a neutral pitch).

To the Teacher:
1. Count one measure before beginning. The Student Workbook has no beginning note or notes given.
2. Have the students sing the exercises back to you as they were played.
3. When the student can sing the exercise accurately he is ready to complete the exercise on paper.

1. Count:

RHYTHM UNIT NO. 16

A. INTRODUCTION OF MIXED METER AND REVIEW OF PREVIOUS MATERIAL

To the Student: The teacher will play a short rhythmic exercise. The first measure of each exercise is completed for you.

Directions: Complete the rhythm of the exercise on a neutral pitch. These exercises contain changes in meter. Be sure to mark the new meter at the beginning of the first bar in which it is used.

To the Teacher:
1. Play the exercise once or twice.
2. Have the students immediately tap or say the exercise back exactly as you played it. If the exercise is too long for this, divide it into sections.
3. When the students have accurately memorized the exercise, they are ready to write their answers on paper.

THE FIRST MEASURE OF EACH EXERCISE IS GIVEN IN THE STUDENT WORKBOOK.

RHYTHM UNIT NO. 16

Workbook Page 225

B. REVIEW

To the Student: Below is a series of rhythmic exercises. In each exercise the notation will agree with the dictated version except on ONE beat only.

Directions: Circle the number indicating the beat which is *not* played as notated.

To the Teacher: Since the problem involved in this set of exercises is a matter of selection rather than dictation, the speed of these exercises may be increased considerably.

*Indicates the beat which disagrees with the Workbook version.

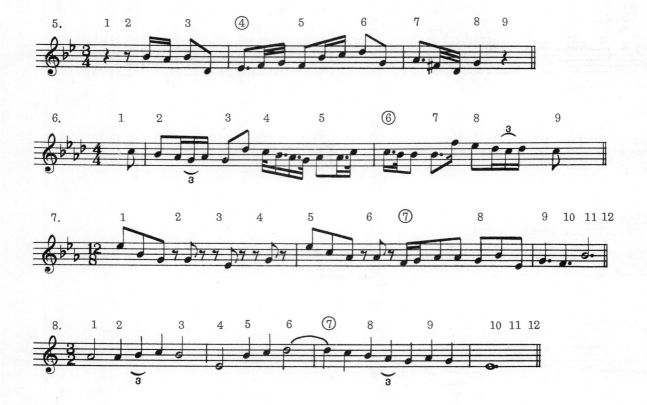

Workbook Page 226

RHYTHM UNIT NO. 16

C. MORE DIFFICULT EXERCISES

To the Student: In these exercises no beginning notes are given to help you. The instructor will count one measure before beginning each exercise.

Directions: Write the rhythm on the staff in notation (use a neutral pitch).

To the Teacher:

1. Count one measure before beginning. The Student Workbook has no beginning note or notes given.
2. Have the students sing the exercises back to you as they were played.
3. When the student can sing the exercise accurately he is ready to complete the exercise on paper.

1. Count:

2. Count:

3. Count:

4. Count:

5. Count:

6. Count:

7. Count:

8. Count:

TAPES TO ACCOMPANY WORKBOOK IN EAR TRAINING

REEL NO.	UNIT TYPE	UNIT NO.	SECTION	EXERCISE NUMBERS
1	MELODY	1	A	1, 3, 6, 10, 13
			B	1, 2, 8, 10, 12
			C	1, 3, 6, 15, 16
			D	1, 2, 3, 4, 5, 11, 12, 13, 14, 15, 31, 32, 33, 34, 35, 51, 52, 53, 54, 55
		2	A	1, 5, 6, 8, 10
			B	1, 5, 6, 7, 8
			C	1, 5, 16, 27, 34
			D	1, 2, 3, 4, 5, 21, 22, 23, 24, 25, 31, 32, 33, 34, 35, 41, 42, 43, 44, 45
			E	1, 2, 3, 4, 11, 12, 13
2		3	A	1, 5, 14, 15, 22
			B	1, 4, 10, 11, 12
			C	1, 6, 14, 21, 41
			D	1, 2, 3, 4, 5, 11, 12, 13, 14, 15, 31, 32, 33, 34, 35, 41, 42, 43, 44, 45
		4	A	1, 12, 16, 19, 21
			B	1, 4, 6, 7, 8
			C	1, 13, 15, 45, 47
			D	1, 2, 3, 4, 5, 11, 12, 13, 14, 15, 31, 32, 33, 34, 35, 41, 42, 43, 44, 45, 51, 52
3		5	A	1, 6, 8, 18
			B	1, 7, 14, 22
			C	1, 3, 7, 15
			D	1, 2, 3, 4, 5, 11, 12, 13, 14, 15, 31, 32, 33, 34, 35, 41, 42, 43, 44, 45
		6	A	1, 8
			B	1, 2, 3, 10, 11, 16, 17
			C	1, 9, 11, 19, 29
			D	1, 2, 3, 4, 5
4		7	A	1, 5, 17
			B	1, 5, 7
			C	1
			D	1, 2, 3, 4, 5, 21, 22, 23, 24, 25
		8	A	9, 10
			C	1, 4, 7, 12
			D	1, 2, 3, 4, 5, 11, 12, 13, 14, 15, 41, 42, 43, 44, 45

REEL NO.	UNIT TYPE	UNIT NO.	SECTION	EXERCISE NUMBERS
4	MELODY	9	A	1, 5, 6
			B	1, 7, 18, 20
			C	1, 4
			D	1, 2, 3, 4, 5, 11, 12, 13, 14
5		10	A	1, 2, 3, 4
			B	1, 4, 11
			C	1
			D	1, 2, 3, 4, 5, 11, 12, 13, 14, 15, 41, 42, 43, 44, 45
		11	A	1, 5, 6
			B	1, 8, 10
			C	1, 5, 7, 11
			D	1, 2, 3, 4, 5, 11, 12, 13, 14, 15
		12	A	1, 5, 6
			B	1, 3, 4
			D	1, 10, 15
6		13	A	1, 2, 11
			B	1, 3
			C	1, 3
			D	1, 5, 11, 15
		14	A	4
			B	1
			C	1
			D	1, 2, 3, 4, 7, 8, 9
		15	A	1, 3
			B	1, 3
			C	1
			D	1, 2, 11
		16	A	4, 5
			B	2
			C	1, 5
			D	1, 2, 10
7	HARMONY	1	A	1, 2, 3, 4, 8, 9, 10
			B	1, 2, 3, 4, 5, 31, 32, 33, 34, 35
			C	1, 2, 3, 4, 5, 16, 17, 18, 19, 20
			D	1, 2, 3, 4, 5, 21, 22, 23, 24, 25
		2	A	1, 2, 3, 4, 5, 6
			B	1, 2, 3, 4, 5, 31, 32, 33, 34, 35
			C	1, 2, 3, 4, 5, 26, 27, 28, 29, 30
			D	1, 2, 3, 4, 5, 11, 12, 13, 14, 15
8		3	A	1, 2, 3
			B	1, 3

REEL NO.	UNIT TYPE	UNIT NO.	SECTION	EXERCISE NUMBERS
8	HARMONY	3	C	1, 2, 3, 4, 5, 6, 7, 8, 9, 10, 21, 22, 23, 24, 25, 26, 27, 28, 29, 30
			D	1, 2, 3, 4, 5, 6, 7, 8, 9, 10, 21, 22, 23, 24, 25, 26, 27, 28, 29, 30
		4	A	1, 2, 3, 4, 5, 6, 7, 8, 9, 10
			B	1, 3
			C	1, 2, 3, 4, 5, 6
			D	1, 2, 3, 4, 5, 6, 7, 8
			E	1, 2, 3, 4
9		5	A	1, 2, 4, 7
			B	1, 4
			C	1, 2
			D	1, 2, 3, 4, 7, 8
		6	A	1, 2, 4, 5
			B	1, 2, 5, 6
			C	1, 2, 3, 4, 5, 6, 7, 8, 9, 10, 16, 17, 18, 19, 20, 21, 22, 23, 24, 25, 31, 32, 33, 34, 35
			D	1, 2, 4, 6
10		7	A	1, 2, 3, 4, 11
			B	1, 3
			C	1, 3
			D	1, 2, 3, 4, 5, 13, 14, 15, 16, 19
		8	A	1, 2
			B	1, 2
			C	1, 2, 3, 4, 5, 21, 22, 23, 24, 25, 31, 32, 33, 34, 35
			D	1, 3
		9	A	1, 3
			B	1, 2, 3, 4, 5, 6, 7, 8
			C	1, 2
			D	1
11		10	A	1, 2, 3
			B	1, 2, 3, 4, 5, 31, 32, 33, 34, 35
			C	1
			D	2, 3, 4, 5, 6
		11	A	1, 3, 5, 10
			C	1
			D	1, 2, 3, 4, 5, 21, 22, 23, 24, 25
		12	A	1, 2

REEL NO.	UNIT TYPE	UNIT NO.	SECTION	EXERCISE NUMBERS
11	HARMONY	12	B	1, 2, 3, 4, 5, 11, 12, 13, 21, 22
			C	2, 3, 4, 5
		13	A	1, 2, 3, 4
			B	1
			C	1, 2, 3, 4
			D	1, 2, 11, 12
12		14	A	1, 2, 3, 4
			B	1, 2, 6
			C	1, 2, 7, 8
			D	1, 2, 3, 7
		15	B	1, 5
			C	1, 3
			D	1, 2, 3, 4, 5, 6, 7, 8, 9, 10
		16	A	2, 3, 6
			B	1, 2, 3, 4, 5, 11, 12, 13, 14, 15, 21, 22, 23, 24, 25
			C	2, 3
			D	1, 6, 7
13	RHYTHM	1	A	1, 2, 3, 4, 13, 14, 19, 20
			B	1, 2, 5, 6, 9, 10, 12
			C	1, 3, 7, 8, 9
		2	A	1
			B	1, 2, 15, 16
			C	1, 2, 3
		3	A	1, 10, 12
			B	13, 14
		4	A	1, 7
			B	1, 4, 10, 12
			C	1
		5	A	1, 2, 3, 4, 5
			B	1, 7
		6	A	1, 2, 3, 4
			B	1, 7
			C	1, 6
		7	A	1, 9, 13, 15
			B	1, 8
			C	1, 8
14		8	A	1, 2
			B	1, 2, 7, 8, 18, 19
		9	A	1, 5, 7, 9, 10
			B	1, 2, 6, 11, 12
		10	A	1, 2, 3, 4, 13, 14, 15
			B	1, 4, 8
			C	1, 2
		11	A	1, 2, 3
			B	1, 8
		12	A	1, 5
			B	1, 5, 6, 8

REEL NO.	UNIT TYPE	UNIT NO.	SECTION	EXERCISE NUMBERS
14	RHYTHM	13	A	1, 2, 9, 10
			B	1
			C	5
		14	A	1
			B	1
			C	1
		15	A	1
			B	1
			C	5
		16	B	1

TEACHER'S DICTATION MANUAL
IN
EAR TRAINING